# I'M-MIGRANT

*A collection of Poems*

by

*Dwight Maxwell*

First Printing, 2019
**ISBN:** 9798386723033

For permission requests, write to the publisher, addressed "Attention:
Permissions Coordinator," at the address below.


273 The Broadway,
Dudley, DY1 3DP

Email address: tafariacademy@gmail.com

https://linktr.ee/DwightMaxwell

## *Dedication*

*I dedicate this book of poems to my family and friends, who supported and encouraged me to share my poetry with the world. May the words of these pages resonate with your hearts and minds and uplift your spirits.*

*Gyn Nyame*
*If not for God…*

## Table of Contents

*My Rasta cousin died in the woods*

My Rasta cousin died in the woods of Clarendon, in the district of Morse.
He lived in a half finished house made with grey cinder blocks and steel.
Cutting brown shapes on thick green leaves—
He abandoned the half-walled house because he said he was a Rasta man.

Rasta man don't use comb or eat pork.
Rasta man don't brush teeth, or walk street.
Rasta man chew chew-sticks and drink cerasee tea.
Rasta man grow dreadlocks and live off ackee tree.

My Rasta cousin's mother is Aunty Adasa, a young
round face woman, smooth black black skin,
and a voice as smooth as alabaster, a smooth liquor
to warm your throat.  He was her only son.  He worshipped the Bible
wore it on his hips like a loaded gun.

My Rasta cousin ate the jungle raw, ingested
ganja through his pores, and Haile Selassie I appeared onto him
with feet of burnished bronze and hair of lamb's wool– so he left home
headed into the hills to a commune of Rastafari
leaving the mystery of Babylon behind.

My Rasta cousin wore the island like his clothes.
Back into the raw earth, naked like Adam before the Fall.
The Banyan was his shade, the aphrodisiac of the papaya
Sending him high and deep into the layer of mother Nature.

Rasta man don't drink white rum or shoot gun.
Rasta man chants peace and love.
Rasta man chants down Babylon into the ground.
Rasta man shakes his natty-dread and smokes sinsemilla.

My Rasta cousin sleeps in the bush, like an owl on a branch so still he looked.
In the quarters of Duppy and rolling calf he slept.
Ol' Hige and River Mumma discussed his fate.
Her cackles heard from miles away.

My Rasta cousin survived off leaves, like a goat in a field.
He didn't eat salt, cooked ital food live and direct from the land.

He was a Bongo man, beating his drum until morning come.
He trod like a Natty Dread burning all FEDs and Bald heads.

So when I heard that my cousin was dead—a raven brought the news
from the bushes of Morse. They said he died of starvation.
For months, the forest had fed my Rasta cousin like an offspring
and now it turned against him like an unforgiving parent…
whipped him, scolded him for lifting her veil.
Now she marched him into thorns as he searched for the repellent herb.

Rasta man don't drink white rum or shoot gun.
Rasta man chants peace and love.
Rasta man chants down Babylon into the ground.
Rasta man shakes his natty-dread and smokes sinsemilla
all day long until he falls fast asleep under banyan tree.

*A letter to our children abroad*

### I

There's turmoil in Maypen, Montego Bay,
Rock River— in Kingston, cardboard and tin
shacks lined the streets. A pacing mother begs
for a teaspoon of salt to cook her dinner
        a baby on her tilted hip.
The red-faced newborn cried like a kitten
hunger marked in the lines on his face.

"You can't tighten yu belt no tighter..
bwoy dem wicked Sah!" voiced a Rasta
with freshly made brooms balancing on his head,
riding by the queue of shoppers
waiting desperately outside Mr Chung's greasy shop.
Shopkeepers married goods.
It was either flour or rice with a bottle of Dettol
or you didn't eat that night.

"Come mek we go a ground go plant peas and carn."
Hoes and pickaxes slanted on shoulders
of haggard farmers, who ploughed harsh fields with scowling faces.
Backs broken in silence as planting songs echoed
in the humid, hot, howling air under a crystal clear sky:

*"Gó dung a Immanuel road gal an bwoy*
*fi gó bruck rock stone!*
*Gó dung a Immanuel road gal an bwoy*
*fi gó bruck rock stone!"*

At times even the air works against them
starving their lungs as they bend into the ground.
Pick axes cut neat slices in the air
deep gashes opened up in the stubborn ground.

*"Bruck dem one by one, gal an bwoy!*
*Bruck dem two by two, gal an bwoy!*
*Finger mach no cry, gal an bwoy*

The blazing Jamaican sun forced the hungry
men and boys to retreat and unclench the pickaxes they swung

from moon-set to moon-rise (as the blood
stains and calluses in their palms were ignored).
Uncle Manley ordered me to drop the gunga peas and corn
into the gaping holes in the earth as I strolled behind him,
head down.

*"Memba a play we deh play, gal an bwoy!*
*Memba a play we deh play, gal an bwoy!*
*Finga 'mash no cry, gal an bwoy..*

## II

The women here have denied the land nothing,
but these are hard times. The earth
still would not fill their baskets. Ackee, pimentos,
breadfruit, pear and even yam was scarce.
The land just will not give them a thing.
Even the sweat of their brows brought no bread.

*"Sammy plant piece a carn dung a gully,*
*an it bare till it kill poor Sammy.*
*Sammy dead! Sammy dead! Sammy dead O!"*

Once there was an intruder in our fields
when the ground was dry and cracked like thunder.
He left no clues behind. The well was dry; Aunt Hetti cried
for she was tired of making cassava dumplings.
Uncle Manley used the swivel-jack[1] to interrogate
us and it broke in the drought. I don't believe
that we were all innocent. We were all prowlers
in some vague nefarious manner— roaming the silent bush
in search of fruits to quench our hunger.
Come dawn we began to plant again.
Uncle Manly chased mi round de yard
with a switch in his big black farmer's fist.
I ran like a mongoose in a sugarcane field
defiant and strong with hungry lips.

*"Who say Sammy dead? A who say Sammy dead?*
*Him no dead O. A lie dem a tell. A rumour dem a spread."*

---

[1] *A cane used to spank children in the 80s*

III

Tired of coal stoves and kerosene lamps.
The children of the land of wood and water
abandoned their homes in Point Hill, Pusey Hill
and Maypen. Markets stalls were offering nothing.
Jesus fed the poor cassava dumplings and chicken back,
whilst the rich in Kingston ate ackee and salt-fish.
The countryside was an abandoned ruin,
a lone donkey with wooden hampers
meandered down a desolate road.
Families packed up and left for Town
like a herd of zebras migrating to a new watering hole.
There were many casualties
along the arduous passage to Kingston Town.
Hunger had robbed them of all their senses.
Majestic green mountains exchanged
for swanky ghettos— shacks after shacks
were all your eyes could see.
And the choking stench of gutters in your throat
perfumed the huddled silence of regret.

*"Who say Sammy dead? A who say Sammy dead?*
*Him no dead O. A lie dem a tell. A rumour dem a spread*
*Sammy run gone left the living dead O."*

Page 15

*Pusey Hill, Jamaica before the flood*

In her brown soapy water
is a disappearing town
where fever-grass dries
crackling in tongues

she will stoop by a wash pan
and become old

a full stone

and as I appear like a dressed-down American,

her heavy toil transforms into suds

dirt is exorcised
she hangs diadems out to dry

stones in the heat prophesied
as the cassavas dried
            peppers twang in the heat
the dry well's hollow promises
are as enticing as the ones I carried from America
to soothe her aching back

mango season erupted and left the land barren

I found remnants of her household
the latest fossils to be realised
before leaving for America

her long fingers caressed the children's clothes
a few pieces of her own she has laid out to dry
upon ancestral grave stones.

*Bigger's Boys*

The sun, sinking by the Blue Mountains' embrace,
Interferes with life, in its smallest trace.
Grassy fields recline, hips to the ground,
Elbows and groves in benediction found.

Emerging from pimento trees and redwood's might,
Bigger's boys appear, like shy goats taking flight.
Words of love exchanged, urging one another on,
Gadflies and wood beetles, their presence condoned.

A hill of fresh coal, cooling in tranquil ease,
Red dirt blankets, soothing the black bricks' tease.
Splinters fly, as coals are carefully broke,
Raking the ground, freeing heat's smoky cloak.

Sacks filled lazily, under hot Jamaican sun,
In the dry open air, the brothers' work is done.
Longing for maternal love, absent in their days,
Hidden in the burning bush, its enigmatic ways.

Or perhaps in the lonesome nights, Shanti Bush's domain,
Terror-filled bedtime, waiting for Bigger's wrath to profane.
Children's laughter dances freely in the breeze,
Toil ceases, as the eldest prepares the feast with ease.

Dumplings, sardines, yellow yam's delight,
Scotch bonnet peppers, tomatoes ripe and bright,
Sweet potatoes, memories of years gone by,
A potion to cherish, as time wanders nigh.

Angels beckon, Peace embraces their souls,
Midday sky blazes, reuniting it consoles.
Rapture soothes the boys, as sleep claims its reign,
In the wings of reunion, dreams remain.

*Brothers*

My mother fled Jamaica, back when I was just a young one,
Incognito, beneath stars, in cool nightshade's skin, she'd run.
Now she resides in the Big Apple, hustling to break her chains,
Day and night, grinding hard, striving for greater gains.

Uncle sold me out for his own freedom, a twisted obeah man,
Running errands, trapped in his grip, life not going as planned.
School barely touched, my education left undone,
Labouring the land, missing out on the learning fun.

Strong and sun-kissed, my skin bears the mark,
Climbing mountains like a goat, leaving my imprint in the dark.
But beneath it all, my soul brims with love's embrace,
For my brother, I'd give my all, in any time or place.

A knight he became, confronting the wicked obeah spell,
I played my gentle role, guiding him through life's hell.
I caressed his woolly head, watched him graze on knowledge's page,
But oftentimes misunderstood, our bond tested in a fiery rage.

In wars, he'd stand against me, misjudging my heart's call,
Yet deep down, I know he loves me, from days of yore's.
When brothers gathered wood for coal, water on heads along burning roads,
I released my grasp on him, like a slippery toad he goes.

Fast and bold, thorny and tough, my brother went his own way,
But the love remains, for our bond nothing can truly betray.

Page 19

*The woman who was not grandmother*
*For my adopted grandmother, known as Mother B to the living*


My grandmother was not really my grandmother.
She who took me in when I had no other
Was naught to me but a stranger smelling of cornmeal and sugar.
O' the woman I called, my grandmother is not at all a kin of mine.

She is a Syrian woman washed up from bottom of the sea
Barnacles hanging from her Asian hair.
She told tales of a father, a dark blue-skinned African
With beetle eyes, who spilled his seed out of lost in the ocean night
In sorrow for his kinfolk lives, who from the dry cliffs of Syria
took supernatural flight.

The woman I called my grandmother was patroness of the thread.
She peddled folk songs and sew three-sister dresses to pay the rent.
Full of pride, my eyes could not deny that I loved her rosy cheeks
Her young fingers weaving colours for little girls who danced at church.

My grandmother pedals me to sleep—something new to wear when I wake.
In the hot days we baked together in the sun picking breadfruits,
some unearthly papaya fills her skirt
like heads of children she never birthed, such gentle breast un-milked,
and those maternal instincts she could not in-still in me.

She fed me and told me stories of her Syrian eyes and her Syrian skin,
And I listen softly like a sick cherub doting on his unnatural birth,
Longing to be her sole apprentice and most of all, to relive her tales.
She spun threads into my breast teaching me the vowels of Syrian love.

*Return to Jamaica 7/2022*

*Moneague*

The hill people, a distant memory now faded from my mind. Moneague's narrow streets raced alongside the humpback king, their voices escaping as we passed through. These mountains, once distant, were now within my grasp. This return, like the others, held a solemn beauty, a revelation that transcended the ordinary. I gazed beyond myself, peering over ridges that stretched along the road, the mountains sluggishly trailing behind.

These mountains carried the weight of abundance, possessing everything expected of them. It felt as if I journeyed through the belly of a snake, winding and twisting through its insides, slowly being digested. Willingly surrendering, I let my guard down, placing my camera at my feet. Above and below me, the precarious homes of the hill people stood. I marvelled at the slopes and angles they navigated, their bare feet clinging to the ground like magnets on a refrigerator.

They adapted, leaning to accommodate the mountain, walking parallel or perpendicular to the air, gliding through thin bamboo trees. Wherever there were no plains to settle upon, they found ways to walk upright, sitting outdoors on warm, polished steps of red. The ways of the mountain, what secrets do they hold? Do the people of Moneague recite verses about her mysteries? How many may have stumbled, rolling to the mountain's feet, sinking into the Earth's embrace, into the bauxite-red dirt that splashes against the narrow road, like blood flowing from deep lacerations on the skin's surface.

From yonder store atop the hill's crest,
A relic of masters, bricks sagged, unrest,
Their aged skin mirroring bygone days,
Summoned by the bus on Mandeville's winding ways.

Rolling past the crone, tending goats serene,
Her wandering herds, a meditative scene.
Where potent rum flows, men rise and fall,
Bible pages lay siege, tales upon verandahs sprawl.

Women and children scurry, long-lost fathers await,
Waving in welcome, as if to abate,
The absence of departed troops, battles fought,
Reunion, a bittersweet victory sought.

Kerosene lamps, nonchalant on windowsills,
Darkened woods yearn for pickaxes, ploughing thrills,
Barren cupboards longing for bounty's stay,
Tin mackerels, sardines, Kool-Aid's array.

Bulla cakes and sacks of rice they lug,
Cooking oil by barrels, fish maw for stray cats, a hug.
Hymns of abundance, now joyously sung,
In the red earth, sorrel's blood is wrung.

In distant valleys, perpetual hymns resound,
Pinnacled churches, aged, twilight-bound.
Pastor leads the herd, baptisms in the river's embrace,
Timbrels and palms serenade with grace.

Fathers wheeled their aproned wives in pleated attire,
From Mandeville to Victoria Town, desires aspire.
Congested with wares, Kingston's bounty they bring,
Coal miners with sooty eyes, soaping in mud's sting.

Enamel basins summon the weary home,
Dirty-boy soaps, tender bricks, an earthly tome.
Hopes of a hilly town coalesce in frames,
Maypoles, ring games, and family's trades claim.

Outside the stumbling bus, men cling like ants
Pirates on masts, swinging, taking daring chance,
Recklessly dangling from iron chariot's sails,
Bound where mariners fear, astride the bus quivering frame.

Oh, reader, they venture where dangers lurk,
Careless in their innocence, some to the city err.
The country bus, packed tight, rafters groan,
Strangers' thoughts heard, as skins rub in moans.

Through haze-filled vistas, on candle's fading light,
Mandeville to Kingston, their journey's delight.
As night's curtain falls, a solitary door's creak,
A farmer kisses his wife, parting sorrows they speak.

Sacks of coal neatly piled, sturdy rows align,
The bus stops, a runaway steps inside.

## Yam Communion

Beneath the vast expanse, the sun's tempest swells,
While the gracious woman tends her baskets' weight,
Between her iron limbs, apron stained and worn,
A cradle sways, embracing sleepy brown skin.

Today, I purchase my first piece of yam,
The Earth's own salt, the staff that sustains life.
In pure water, I shall cook this humble root,
A communal offering for the town to share,
Where yams shall sprout and flourish in my neighbour's' plots.
Through this gesture, my love and hope take root,
And perhaps they'll honour me with words of praise,
Gather in celebration to savour the taste of yams.
Within their hearts, the love they sense will grow,
Supporting causes nestled in secret folds.

Toothless smiles, the proudest tokens of joy,
The woman grasps my calloused hand, imbuing it with her service.
Together, we choose the yams, tender as a midwife's touch,
Placing them gently in my hamper, their earthy embrace.
"Here is how you'll cook them," she softly murmurs,
Kneeling amidst folds akin to Saint Teresa's grace,
Her presence a breeze that lifts my weary spirit.
I can almost taste the curry on her fingers,
The fragrant spices that adorn her being,
As I kneel, humbled, to honor ancestral spirits,
Seeking their blessing upon this sacred feast.

*Farewell to home (Jamaica)*

We left our Jamaican home, guided by mother's plan,
Braided hair, born years ago, in Kingston's tenement land.
Streets sown with shattered glass, aftermath of revolution's fight,
Kerosene lamps glowing, torch-like, casting a fragrant light.

Ancient Bible pages adorned our humble abode,
Like hopeful palms, awaiting blessings from Jesus, bestowed.
While we slept, Psalms were whispered, keeping spirits at bay,
Guarding against duppy, Obeah man, and ghosts that may stray.

A family mismatched, brought together by destiny's hand,
Strangers turned aunts, uncles, cousins, a united band.
Neighbours shared tales of political battles, Seaga vs Manley.
We tasted their rations, playing our roles in the political chase.

Jones Town's memory lingers, their smells and burning homes,
Seeking new paths, as coloured people, no longer bound by zones.
Escaping black hell's clutches, breaking free from suffering's hold,
Leaving behind poverty's fruits, devoured by worms, untold.

Behind red-smeared cinder blocks, we built bridges anew,
Mother cleaned offices, a better life came into view.
In the capital, a bigger house we could afford,
Fictitious kinship remained, threads of connections ignored.

We learned to savour each meal, not rush as if it's the end,
Knowing tomorrow brings more, our hunger won't offend.
No assassins lurked on our streets, no hunger's deadly touch,
Unlike the regretful thrusts that consumed lives too much.

So we danced, like runaway slaves seeking a promising fate,
Arriving in Nanny Town, with dreams we couldn't abate.
Colonists' deceptive rhymes enticed us from our shores,
To Harlem, Queens, and Brooklyn's ghettos, new chapters in store.

Meeting uncles and cousins in prisons of inequality,
Red graffiti promised more, cloaking the truth with audacity.

*Another Night (from my mothers diary)*

The lackadaisical scent of tobacco is the sweat of the earth.
The steady stride of Okimbo Alingua,
my captious father,
the mulatto god

whose brown fists planted seeds
into the belly of our land.
I'm still too slow for those impossible strides
still too blind to witness my mother's hands in the darkness.

She who masqueraded as night
as her basket of food sways
upon her head, recites the liturgy of a foreign
Eucharist in the Parish church deep in Clarendon.

They said my father's mother saw a ghost,
took it inside her and lived. My father's thin melanin
is proof of this consternating story.

Don't throw stones at night, my father said,
you might hit the moon's secret eyes
or something dead standing near by.

I loved horses, my father owned a few.
He would approach me at full gallop, a Moorish grin
on the face he reserved for me, to pluck me from the ground
his white nails like stars digging into my side,
taking me for a joy ride in the lush Clarendon hills.

I was a black Persephone, my father was my uncle
every time he scooped me from the red dirt.
We too riding to our deaths
my mother waved, emphasis on her smile.

*Beneath the monarch's wings*

And she departed from herself, akin to a monarch butterfly,
Emerging in spring from a cocoon's embrace.
Wandering through bustling streets, she tasted
All that the farmers brought, a sensory feast.
Her colors unfurled, scattering like confetti,
Merging with the folds and creases of the sea.
I could not reach her, never glimpsed her dark eyes,
As she acquired the captured creatures of the waves.

A new dress fashioned from yellow calico,
Carried the fragrance of her warm perspiration,
And the crowded bus she boarded for the town.
The dress sang upon her form in the marketplace,
Her daughter by her side, a little nymph in tow,
Tracing the graceful steps of her mother's dance.
Bright as a lemon among a sea of limes,
Her baskets burdened with red snappers,
Doctors and porgy fish concealed by paper and brittle ice.

She hoisted the child's weight for the first time,
Kneeling to ease the burden upon her own,
Like an ancient woman drawing water from the Nile,
For the sake of divine felines and sacred rites.
Her countenance bore the semblance of Nubian wood,
A weathered mask, imbued with ancestral power,
Wood that had witnessed tarnished ceremonies.

Her neck swayed beneath the weight, shifting from right to left,
Left to right, seeking equilibrium and poise.
And so, grandmother, you strode away from that harbour,
With fleeting concerns, convinced of harmony's hold,
As if you carried the entire scene within you,
Embodied in the monarch's wings,
Taking it all along on the journey home, aboard the country bus.

*The exile*

In the Caribbean sun's blazing heat,
I buried my toes in sand so sweet.
Becoming one with waves and songs,
Seabirds twirling, where memories are abandoned.

Gardens of hibiscus kites from days of yore,
Gifts of breadfruit and ackee on my mother's shore.
Forgotten memories sparked anew,
Like a Christian baptised in ocean's blue.

Voices echoed from a distant reef,
Souls of slaves lost in history's grief.
Sailors and pirates once roamed this place,
Sunday's high noon, a lively embrace.

Black Beard's tales and a wooden leg's beat,
Late night gatherings where pirates would meet.
A church nearby, its bell pealing high,
Sinners praying in tongues, brothers to the sky.

Venetian sea danced to hymns within,
As I bid farewell to the golden table's sin.
The island begged me not to depart,
But I turned from her, aching for a fresh start.

The American dream, across distant seas,
Unrest in my soul, a longing to roam free.
New York beckoned, its allure so deep,
Glancing back at the sea, for memories to keep.

Wondering if true freedom I'll ever see,
Leaving behind home, uncertain what will be.

## The mythical white woman

All morning you sit and write middle class poems
constructed like a paper mâché.
My fingers caress the words you left on the plates
dirty saucers and cups, an eye sore in the sun.
Your guests pontificate as you showed them the way
to the living room for tea and cakes.

Your middle-class poems are like prune trees
on a manicured lawn with rocks sculpted by the fit gardener
you instructed in his daily routine: "everything must be
in their proper places—balance is everything."
You believe Betty Crocker is a reality Stainless steel,
ornate pictures frames enshrined long deceased pets—
the only real people left in your skit.

Even Martha Stewart is real to you.
In your sunflower apron, wide-brimmed skirt
with matching shoes and stockings, you wheeled around in your kitchen
placing your Tupperware in pairs, as if they were born of you—
something organic. Perhaps they published you in Poetry
because your verses are so goddamn plastic-realistic.
Your place is assured in the hierarchy of the suburb.

I left crumbs of my world in a news article about Floyd
on the table for you to inspect so you could see
the worlds I breathe when you are walking your poodle.
I am going with the guests. But before I leave, let me tell you,
your kitchen is culture-less. The loud odour of the pastel tiles.
Your dishes have never truly experienced life—
and the house trained wives
            enjoyed every morsel of it.

Somehow Ms. Mary went to bed.
Television was left on.
"Eternal father bless our land…"
JBC signing off.
Lukewarm light dallied from off street
through window curtains.
Full bed and floor mat,
and all the while television's humming
in the delinquent dark.

Donavon falls off the roof
whispered bionic verses through the air.
Hard dough bread and cheap coca tea,
four heads on one pillow,
the growl of a mangy dog
outside of the house near the television.

White noise drowns us in our sleep.
Beyond the white noise a black god
strokes a mountain in a black pool.
How this old woman can break up her body
into so many folds, I don't know.
Night brings her slowly to the couch
by the door, a sleeping Sentinel,
door creeks at her ear.

Rub her shoulder now with some Vicks.
She left the television aghast—white noise—
one million ants gnawing at the brain.
A man falls after a hale of bullets
and his head shatters on the pavement.

Cranky feet from working long in de restaurant.
Flesh and bones fixed in unnatural postures—
Sometimes the bus takes unfamiliar places in night.
Empty side walks, a quiet thing
a world reveal piece by piece,
the light from dark corneas.
Familiar land marks are seen in unspoken visions

softly, O so softly she treads home by the zincs.

When the light flicks on a 12:30 am
terrible feelings let sorrow and joy capitulate,
as handbag, stockings and apron slams to the floor
as one before my half sleepy corneas, black exuding light—
television grabs the iris like a lover, and Mother's
pupils and the white-noise met over sleeping children.

Toes bent like ten old women bent over a river
hot evening and mosquitoes bother eyes and ears
every hit is a miss.  Smell of work in hair and face,
eyes and fingers.  Bed creeps into nightgown.
Sleep closes eyes and dreams—encapsulates
one room in a figure, in a figure of struggle.

Page 32

## The wind and crow

Would you fly with me tonight?
Said the wind to the resting Crow.
The cornfield's barren
And the moon wants affection

So will you fly with me O' Crow
And forget withered corn and bitter snow?
Will you leave behind the empty nest?
Your young yonder gone to rest.

Will you fly abreast with me, if only just to fly?
There is so much to see in Chad
Imagine tea upon golden sands,
Mountains brought low by my insistent hands.

I fly to fill the sails of the humble skiff
On Cuban waves.
I have a child to visit
Who can barely utter his name.

O' Crow, will you hop upon my transparent hair?
Sing perhaps a hymn, no threnodies tonight
No women in cerecloth;
No man wearing blood stains in trenches.

Let's make our beds tonight where turtles bury babes.
I will be still tonight, disturb naught
One flickering light if you come away,
Dear sable Crow, from your lonely scrutiny.

*The Shopkeeper's boy*

"Brother Les is dying behind the tall zinc
go nearly orphaned one
and be like Charon, guide his soul to the shores of Elysium.
Watch his breath, that it passes his lips."
Watch his chest as it heaves

Brother Lest, who builds tall fences,
walks in water boots and raised hogs,
I come to you like Legba on the wind.

The unpainted wooden door swings on one hinge
Like a raided tomb.
Greeted by his moaning, tossing and turning
his clavicle protruding like bridges to the gates of hell.
White bedspreads mummified his flesh
Like sinister sirens, who learned the tongues of men
To lure them into far reaching depths,
so he wept as he swam against the tide of death.

A cloudy interior, hazed his sturdy bed,
Stench of healing balms scented the air.
In this chamber, all words are spells, and dirges
dark winds blow through flickering curtains.
My teenage heart pounced like a steed in my chest
as the dying man began to confess.

Curse that wicked shopkeeper.
Those great hands he ruled me with.
Always wet with penitence and sin.
The words he says that rings me nearly-orphan.
"Yu dirty John crow, come out a mi yard!"

I tended Brother Less's white candles
wiped his sweat as he sipped water
Slipped into his cold black bed to give him company.

The sepulchre of my throat tightens.
How can I sleep next to this dying Brother Less?

It takes courage to sleep next to the dying.
To see a man once strong humbled before the jaws of death.
To hear his rattling breath feeble like a thread.
To hold hands that swallow yours whole,
to utter words to ease the soul.

Brother Less a man of brute strength
Feared among all the little children
that each day saw him march the streets with fierce countenance.
Spills his last words at my little feet
caved in with the calabash house
before the morrow touched the asphalt street.
I cannot remember the words
He gave to me that night, but I know the son that ran away,
Cows neighbours poisoned. I know
His eyes could have encased my body
That parts of me were bargained for, and baited death

Page 36

# A fisherman's tale

*Chorus*

> Pious birds who fed from the boatswain's hands,
> as he sang hymns to the land,
> lend me your feathery lobes, bring idle wings to rest
> on the prows of our colonised lands.
> Beast or man? A howl echoes from cavernous caves.
> Behold he emerged upon the scene, sharp as a wounded knee,
> a shipwrecked stumbling shade, a reluctant prisoner,
> a love sick spirit, who wears the waves like amour.
>
> O' beware! Such a sight is not for the faint hearted.
> Behold I see him gain the favour of a wet wasteland--
> native of this island, native like sand on the beaches of Ocho Rios,
> the home of Paul Bogle ransacked
> on this weird Caribbean isle—we are orphans of the Antilles—
> our island is a junkyard of pirates' skulls and bones.
>
> This was the home of his ancestors, the Ashanti—
> high forehead men who mother-woman bless with rose water
> and bare-rum and coconut oil at birth to prepare them
> for their journey into the arms of the wine dark sea.
> They were hard muscular men, jet black complexion.
>
> On the stolen sand, my father's spirit stares into saffron foam.
> On his shoulder a fishnet, and his face was sun kissed mahogany.
> Leather sandals bound his toes, an old trouser girt his waist.
>
> Silence pelicans! Silence! I bid you..let him speak-- drowned throats
> offer much sorrow and birds cannot contend with sorrow--
> but be still a moment and let him reveal
> the human fiends that doomed him in to this fate.
>
> Tell your story my parent; let the whole world grieve with you!

*Fisherman (painstakingly turning from the sea, wading from the water as if magnetised by it and is being pulled back into it.)*

> Old men are no more dead,
> …unearthed poor Ned from his rest
> let the tongue out of his lungs

to herald its confession.
Pity the sickled moon in my lonesome breast—
I've seen the end my son,
the domain of Pluto is a maze of unbridled pain
and the suffering gathers in me like tulip buds.
My child, these shoulders have not rested
for I must haul these nets even in death
until released by this said sea
whose mourning I placated with verses you taught me.

Many morns over the sea-sprayed-cliffs
I carried you, my only son, to greet the Sun god's eye
and to teach you lineage as only the sun knows.
The sea sported her barnacled robes
and the gay town below woke from its ashes.
Your mother, Josephine, filled my old thermos with Blue Mountain
coffee, sweetened with condense milk and brown sugar.

In the distance I saw the captain of my soul, the warden
of my prison, the ancient sea, glistening like a diamond
as bickering bobbing birds dallied on her rolling flank,
and countless fishermen called out from her—
methought the day unending, tastes of fried crispy snapper
sweet festivals under the stones of Lovers Leap.
Then Tall-man apportioned us rum, filled our lungs
until the day was done.

Ahh, sea who unravels sailors' knots
I summon you now to attend and resurrect the man I was
who rode the shoulders of the waves.
I left my wife and child furlongs behind.
I abandoned the pit of my boat with fishhooks and snares.
Now I alone stand with only the lighthouse as my companion.
But alas, my self-pity is without warrant, my tears hollow.
I alone carried the bulk of the heavy chains
when our shore was carved up like a gutted fish.

We were a school of fishermen of every creed,
but most took the money and the penance that came with it.
They fled the beach, left the shores in desolate mourning.

I would rather drink the salty sea than leave the shores my fathers
left me. I could not fish the sea, I could not roll my net upon the
sand neither could I clean my snares or bait my hooks.
The beach had become sterile they combed it day and night
removed all its vestments and casted them into the wind.
There was no more room for men here. The trees assembled
brave as warriors. But soon they too were hauled down
and in their place constructed Hedonism and Marriotts—
idols permeated the sand, and our coconuts were harvested to feed
burdensome throngs of tourists from foreign lands.

One night I meant to sail my skiff out to sea.
but I came to see it lay mauled like a storm had torn it apart:
my instruments broken, my fishnets casted away no more use to me.
And rage engulfed my senses—an uncontrollable fire ferried me
beneath the indifferent moon. My quarrel spread like a cancer
and rumours of my coming stoked my enemies redress. Their white
flesh trembled at the sight of me —the rednecks
who wore doubled breasted suits even when the sun blazed
like Helios descending into Gia's womb. It came to blows,
they beat me under the howling moon—out of town I ran naked.
I ran for cover in the thicket of the bush. There to lick my wounds
like the dog they had made me into.

In the dire streets your father roamed, disheveled
and induced with sorrow's nectar.
At first I took the homebound path, but the sight of you weeping
made me abandon the course. I fished upon my father's knees
I knew nothing better than the relentless sea, I had no salt--
alas the open sea was all.

It was here I made the final call—on this sea-rock
with its third eye open. Oh, sorrow, you encased me with your
bribery, your spit wallow in me still.
Where is their an edict now—now that death has claimed
the flesh I once owned.
What laws is there that can rival God's own decrees?
The hurricane beats us down, typhoon splits the ship—
Oh merciful God! now all I have is your silent judgment,
your Laws never faded though man may forget his own laws
when it favours him to do so.

*Chorus*

> O' be still, O' soul, the incubus seems to fade, shimmering
> like the sun on the table of the sea. Are those mermaids I see
> coming to take my dear beloved father from me—
> Nearer, nearer still—I mean to know my father's will.
> Reconcile your loses, father, (if I was there you would never have
> plunged). I would have shot them down with my tongue!
> Recall to your mind the usurpers, the men of no land,
> hobbling pirates, bringers of plagues and strife
> whose incursions transformed our fine beaches
> from sacred paradise to hedonistic pleasure—
> dispersed and displaced our kinder-folks like dust in the wind.
> They are the culprit, not you my dearest father,
> not you, O' Saint of the sea, ancient mariner
> who for a millennium sailed from Africa to the Americas.
> Return to your cave, all maladies will ease with dreams.

*Fisherman*

> Too late, too late for to and fro my journeys I learnt the truth--
> No child, Permits are not from God, and I should have lived,
> yet I walked the road to Sheol, and the sin has doomed me—
> a living lighthouse, my eyes reflect the sea. I watch day and night
> for justice with no reprieve.

*Chorus*

> The spirit wanes.
> The sea recalls the spirit to its watery grave.
> The waves rustling blanket to cover mistakes—
> another messenger this way comes.
> Why did you leave me bereft of love?
> The temperance in your fingers made me grasped the pen.
> I am scaled without the shade of your arms.
> Tomorrow, I will bring you psalms to shade your porcelain face.
> Alas the shade evaporates…The sea rolls through his hips
> like wind blowing a gentle white curtain at sunset.
>
> Bobbing birds watch! The ghost repeats the act--
> my father's ghost drinks upon the white sheets of foam
> until at last he is swallowed whole.

*Immigrant farmers beneath the sun*

In the age of dawn, the foreman's decree
Unfurled ancestral lands, bestowed with ease.
He chained us, a dozen souls, beneath the sun's gaze,
With promises as smooth as Adam's first days.
A hundred acres awaited the edge of our toil,
To shed dead trees and vines, the land to uncoil.
Yet the yield proved meagre, a half-acre to share,
For every two men, a fraction, unfair.

Undeterred, we confronted the demiurgic trees,
With saws and axes, we challenged the breeze.
Maidens of twigs and brambles, adorned with brown thorns,
Their eyes howled upon us, their gaze forlorn.
For they laboured, accepting less than fair due,
Their glances measured our sinews, our sinew.

They stooped low, as we climbed their bodies bare,
Unloading our harvest, wrapped with wild care,
In lianas and whips, nature's untamed guise,
Their heads and forms bundled, a captivating guise.
Bending with us, in the moist earth they toiled,
Plowing what we had plowed, with spirits embroiled.
We laughed when Naomi and Ruth sought retreat,
Escaping the sweat and the grass's fierce heat.
We boasted of favour, which maidens we'd choose,
Who yearned to join us once the land was enthused.

Many were daughters of widows, bereft,
Daughters of rivers and streams, long adrift.
A few came to wed us, our trousers to mend,
Rubbing our bellies till sleep would descend.
Each maiden employed her mother's skill and craft,
To hold us, to keep us, their devotion steadfast.

After lunch, the remaining bushes gave way,
Our brides approached, like a burnished wave's sway.
We pursed our lips, arched our backs to the sun,
Chopping, as maidens gathered our sweat, as one.

*My western shack*

Because of patrimony
I hung up my western name neatly
On a hook I found sleeping
In a corner of my house
I undressed in the corner,
Unearthed loose floor boards
And buried my western attire.

I cooked soul soup in the corner
Boiling all my books from the western cannon
I drank the soup passed it out later
In that black-hole corner.

Reclining on my bedroom floor
My arms stretched a mile in opposite directions
Palms tepid, wide open looking at the roof
Naked except for the painful vice around the heels--

I took off my Oxford shoes,
Stretched the sole out on my window sill,
Gave it to the birds.
Looked at my feet torn and callused
My African toes glued together
As if chiseled by Michael Angelou.
I bent down and straighten them out,
Viciously let the air in.

I opened the door of my western shack.
Walked out--- out of my Western mind
gathered fuel from the blood of slaves—
dried up leaves, a discarded noose
Sprinkled them generously through the ad hoc
Of my western living room, kitchen and bathroom.

Then I took two bone white ribs out of my body,
rubbed them till they burnt my skin and flamed the leaves.
My western shack began to burn like a Klan cross
On the manicured lawn of an Anglophile negro.
While the shack burned, I skipped to my desert,
The hyena in me laughing.

In the sheds, we gather 'round,
Eating corn from cans, the sun beats us down.
No more picking apples, let's make our peace,
As the sun sets, protecting us with its golden fleece.
Put away the mallets, no stones to crack,
No more fields of pesticide, we won't look back.
We wait for the first light, the first peace of day,
When birds fill the air, chasing troubles away.

(Chorus)
Oh, old men, warm your hearts with sweet teas,
Water falls from the heavens, blessings on the breeze.
Rest your weary souls, angels draw their swords,
Dream of your loved ones, on distant shores.
Toil must end, a poor man's wage is no recompense,
Be still, my friends, for sleep will bring recompense.
No more death in our eyes, no more broken gates,
We'll rise like the ocean, with coins in our fates.


From their towers, the heirs of empires watch,
Displacing us like sand, with no remorse, no touch.
What cost this brutality, their hearts so cold?
Ignoring prophets' pleas, turning stories untold.
But we won't be silenced, we won't be denied,
With rare birds and kindness, our spirits won't hide.
For we're the ocean men, resilient and strong,
Their indifference won't break us, won't steer us wrong.

(Chorus)
Oh, old men, warm your hearts with sweet teas,
Water falls from the heavens, blessings on the breeze.
Rest your weary souls, angels draw their swords,
Dream of your loved ones, on distant shores.
Toil must end, a poor man's wage is no recompense,
Be still, my friends, for sleep will bring recompense.
No more death in our eyes, no more broken gates,
We'll rise like the ocean, with coins in our fates.

Page 44

(Bridge)
So let the rhythm flow, like waves upon the shore,
In our reggae vibrations, let our spirits soar.
Together we'll rise, united as one,
For justice and peace, our battles won.

(Chorus)
Oh, old men, warm your hearts with sweet teas,
Water falls from the heavens, blessings on the breeze.
Rest your weary souls, angels draw their swords,
Dream of your loved ones, on distant shores.
Toil must end, a poor man's wage is no recompense,
Be still, my friends, for sleep will bring recompense.
No more death in our eyes, no more broken gates,
We'll rise like the ocean, with coins in our fates.

(Outro)
In the face of adversity, we'll stand tall,
With love as our weapon, we'll conquer it all.
No more shed tears, no more despair,
In this reggae revolution, we'll find our share.

*New York Pigeons*

In the bustling city, mornings hum with suffocating hymns,
As residents flow like assembly lines into the rush of traffic,
And trains exhale their weary passengers.

I caught a glimpse of a still lake of words,
Reflecting the tranquility of an early morning.
But the pigeons, my beloved pigeons, no longer perch
Upon my windowsill, their eyes fixed on my tousled face.

Even they have succumbed to urbanisation,
Gentrified like pampered pets of the Lower East Side.
They now inhabit pristine trees, nestled near
Grandiose mansions that loom like prophetic monuments.

They have perky children with cherubic skin,
Who play and frolic with a hint of envy.
Perhaps one day, they too will yearn to be children,
To slip back into their innocent bodies and never know hunger again.

I seldom fed the birds, I confess.
I only noticed their dust and the taint on their wings,
Stirring within me a restless unease.
Aunt Marion from Brooklyn once said,
"New York pigeons are racist," but I cannot fault the birds.

In Harlem, pockets remain undisturbed,
Mansions serve as grim repositories for bodies clad in crack.
Here, prophecies lead to mass suicides,
And the grandeur of those edifices holds little solace.

*Villanelle for my sister*


Something is burning under the little girl's skin.
All those times you said you wanted a boy
You never had a descent man to think.

All those time you planned for a clever boy
And all you gave the girl was in a narrow kitchen
Something is burning under the little girl's skin.

The boy wondered why she threw the red brick at him—
Gave him grief when he did nothing. You told him hit her without mercy.
You never had a descent man to think.

Franky complained that your kids are rowdy
So you packed her things and sent her to Red Hills, not knowing
Something is burning under the little girl's skin.

I sometimes wondered if you would have been smarter, I mean
If you hadn't been brought up without your mother—
You never had a descent man to think.

Where is Frank, and your daughter drowning in her anger?
Your son still conjures up his father when you scold him.
Something is burning under the girl's skin --
You never had a descent man to think.

*For Dubois in Germany*

I've travelled the streets
of Hamburg and Berlin,
and even though I had no hair to comb,
I left a part of me behind.
I've seen how you deconstructed
the Hegelian lies and your superior
intellectual vibes left the German minds in awe.
Some treated you like a man
who had travelled through the centuries,
like Jonah, returning from the belly
of a fish to teach. But I know
you were free there,
just like the straight-billed eagle,
soaring in its kingdom.
The ship tossed and the tides rekindled
the genetic struggles within
the dark hulls of slavery,
a dream you couldn't escape.
How did you feel as all your senses
became one, and the cloven tongue
of a Negro tried to unite?
The double consciousness,
the diabolic dye of America,
splitting you into pieces.
Dubois, I'm here, and I follow close,
with the gait of a sagacious runaway slave.
My gossamer wings are about me now,
and the Proverbs speaks of you and me
as we flee to gather our double selves.
The blue tinctured journey,
the intemperance of the West Wind,
so high and soaring, on white skin
and all its privilege.

*Joy is sorrow unmasked*

Often we know not when sorrow comes
an unexpected knock, a rustle of the wind
a flicker of candle light or a solemn footstep
and sorrow raises her head with news
that comes too late to mend

We know not when sorrow comes
in the afternoon rocking back in your chair
you hear the doorbell announce
an unexpected visitor with a solemn shrug
a sagging brow and a wrinkled face

We know not when sorrow swings upon our gates
sweeps through the pile of autumn leaves
left discarded by a rake where your heart begins to pace
the impolite display, the items knocked down
in your wake, and screams and shouts left unfound

No one knows how the heart at rest begins to race
when sorrow comes to take away the peace
which once you wore like a mascaraed of fate
that joy you claimed would never run away
that joy you served on those days we loved

But sorrow is only a mistress, she doesn't wear the ring
she has no claims to warm hearth stones
that burns bright to warm your voices and your throats
she is a temporary visitor who wears a mask of permanence
behind her stern exterior an empty darkness hushes

Page 50

## A term abroad in Bath, England

In Bristol, the station looms, a colossal barn.
I inhale the pipe's smoke, feeling bold,
Like a tipsy soul on a curb's precipice.
These solitary journeys along miles of steel,
To Bath or wherever my restless feet deem real,
Keep my skin in sync with my beating heart.

"At last," whispered the meek passenger, "England's spell
Is fading." "Indeed," I replied, "It's now
But an island, a dog bereft of its bone."
"Wilberforce our love, no more worship
Like a dove descending from celestial abodes."
My fellow traveler spoke truth,
Yet the newspaper silenced him,
Like tombs of those who championed Empire.

Sour grapes accompany me on the train to Birmingham,
Brooding hours gather in the wake of the breeze,
The present memories woven in the yarn of time,
Tools of masons concealing our pain.
An alka-seltzer tablet soothes heartburn,
It can quell a bird, agitate water,
Tasting like a frosty glass of Pepsi.
But it cannot quench the anguish that afflicts a generation,
Mere erection devoid of gratification,
An illusion of perpetuity and invincibility.

"So, lonely traveler, landscapes are your domain."
Does the sweat on my palm betray me? I set the passport down,
Leaving my bag to evade suspicious gazes,
Untrustworthy bodies and fearful breaths.
I make my way to the water closet.

White fear shadows me: the black man.
I cannot grasp the trigger—I cannot even secure employment.
In the WC— the train halts at Cheltenham Spa.
No one suspects I am an IRA spy, leaving a bomb
Beneath a seat, near a dog, where a woman bends over a book.
But behold, I return to my seat, prepared to perish with them.
I am converted. I believe in the Empire,yet the train must press on.

## Island Man in New York

Within my tongue, words coil like snakes, flesh imbued,
While cockroaches commune near spilled liquid oozed.
Thirst quenched, yet seeing suffering's lament,
This city implored by immigrants who've rent
Their ties to an island existence's haze,
Exiled seekers in the city's dark maze.

Shedding my island binds, at dawn I'll be free?
Untethered, devoid of an insular decree.
The proximity to dreams, a chilling fright,
As we ride the A train into Manhattan's delights,
To seek the pleasures of hell's smoky abyss,
Ulcered conscience rebels, a war I can't dismiss.

Cops, wolves in pursuit, flashlights ablaze,
Jiving to lost poets' rhymes in Judson's haze,
Branding me "no good nigger," they clasp tight,
Interrogation's grip, before releasing with slight
Warning: "Loiter not near religion's affair."
And I dissolve into the bustling street's snare.

Mamma's home, too early from the clinic's hold,
Released by insurance's callous grasp so bold.
Raw blood stains on her sides, healing denied,
Three days unpaid, a callous stride.
Anger deserts, only peace remains,
A bee enamoured by dandelions' refrains.

No justice proclaimed, the beggar within me,
Whom Baldwin cherished, a heartfelt decree.
Ask the street cleaner, purging cyclic grime,
Seek answers in Rwanda's war-etched chime.
Alas, alone I traverse this melting pot's sprawl,
Nutrients boiled, drained from my soul's haul.

Did the island divorce me or did I forsake,
Blue mountains estranged, my heartaches?
Nowhere awaits, withering in my abode,
The Island's son, estranged but not eroded.

## An Evening of Letters

*For Natasha and Larry who died in a car accident during my junior year in college*


To all the trees I have loved in hard times
When soil and snow were unbearable to me,
Fallen leaves dead from grief, clings
To whatever parts of me they can
To deflect the wind that rips into our hearts.
To all the dead things
Of the morning, flying things, things that creep
With crisp iodine wings, craw exposed like beggars.
Crawling things: rodent, small, furred
That greets the dew-damped streets of Harlem
With only their exhale, with only blood
For cats and their extended family --
I have dappled in your eyes with brain-touches.
Pity is born from cock-eyed stares…
I fein tabula rasa as I braced for stench of urine and faeces
As the 'crackhead' hobbled towards me with outstretched arms
Staggering through the dog shit of eternal dogs that roam St. Nicholas
But not at night, at least not in the same manner
As she trod upon the early morning stench,
Through the quick-silver blood of the rain, ice picks from heaven
causing me to wake early and hard for nothing.

To everything that I have heard sigh and ease
And bares the sorrow of Harlem's mother at sunset
As birds herald seeds and worms upon the icy currents in cheeks of steel
So working mothers carry seeds from pale palms for chicks like fierce owls.
Children hugged legs like fog-beings
Between the thighs and cupboard doors.
The tears are enough to wipe the Spanish army out.

To all the evenings, God does not touch us
And does not bother to find us -- pray!!
Pray over cocaine and cold beer, and the last sniff
Will still be the first and stick with you forever.

Evenings without reprieve, two blocks beyond

The church sings.
Evenings I scurried up to Harlem like a doctor
On call in snow, the patient dies every time
And the door is always left ajar for me...
The Victim's family stares and forgives
Every evening feeds you and lets you scurry on home.

So many nights without love or grace
No time for communal love from church and state.
No time to plant kisses onto stiff necks.
Moving along on the rim of pain in rainy weather,
My stomach stink with acid put there by Stygian fingers.
My body folds into Harlem's sorrows.

I come home to the cries of an ancient woman
Who threatens to tie her belly
and wear sackcloth to punish disobedient children.
She makes me see the lover who I killed with sex;
Sex that men cultivate to give women to earn the right to live.
O' room that moved with rhythms of my single bed
Her black body sweating into my eyes.
I howled for days afterwards up into the uterus of the sky
Begging birds to bare me up from my crime against her sacred vagina
From my foolish manly vice.
My rigid body turning with new eyes:
the woman uses her warm fingers to cover
The eye that was wounded by Set.

Page 55

## Runaway Slave

At sunrise's call, mountains softly sigh,
Whispering psalms to birds that traverse the sky.
With each chirp, a rebirth, a fresh morning's birth,
My hope awakens, stirred by their songs' mirth.

From a slumber drenched in intoxicating sleep,
I cry out, a restless prisoner, my soul's aggrieved.
A runaway of the second generation, set free,
Yet bound by the chains of double consciousness, I see.

In the distance, torches ignite, burning bright,
Faces disfigured, contorted by the fiery light.
Men holler, canines howl, sprinting ahead of night,
Their barks recount tales to covetous seekers of my life.

A trail of sweat foreshadows my impending fate,
An endless cotton field, stained by screams innate,
My voice muted, my throat silenced by pain's hold,
As I navigate this labyrinth, both harrowing and bold.

Nowhere to flee, Oh Lord, I gave my all,
Seeking refuge amidst the swamp's murky sprawl,
To evade the crucifix, ravenous and cruel,
Betrayed, I find solace in the lamentation's fuel.

The noose tightens its grip upon my soul's flight,
An effigy, ascending through the smoky night,
My reflection mirrored in their unyielding gaze,
Prayers tremble upon my lips, a solemn praise.

In that moment, atop Mount Calvary's steep crest,
Jesus' blood intertwines, mingling with my oppressed chest.
A fusion of sacrifice, a shared crimson flow,
I bear witness to redemption's painful tableau.

## The Dawn Motel (St. Nicholas Ave, NY)

Outside the Dawn motel I stood.
Outside I saw death fly by ignoring souls pleading to die.
I have confessions for birds,
For twigs and bottles.
The air reeked of holy sinners
brewing strange currents of possibilities
For sins not yet recorded.

My heart sinks within my chest
my lungs linger longingly at the forbidden fruit
each step sure secure to sin,
a commandment broken
with luscious relish.

While I stood in front of the Dawn
Motel, full and confident in my budding
Youthful hunger for love, for pain
for belonging, to enter what was profane
not knowing what would be lost or gained
where men emerge with swaggering steps
and women with coy grins and foxy trots.

Dawn motel Saint of sin
displays her wares on St. Nicholas Ave,
in Harlem's harem she solemnly glances.
In the depths of hours she silently summons.

2.
Has my lust consumed me?
Am I mistaking my desires for destiny?

"All hail reveller. Hail son of Lilith."
"What manner of creatures are these
that dares address me with such beguiling greetings
so withered and so wild in their attire?—
They look like women,
but their serpentine forms
forbid me to see them as such.
Chimeras or gorgons?

come to lure men to their deaths.
"Live you?"

3.
transfixed behind a blank staring door,
a room build for pleasure and nothing more
images and forms of uncountable delectable sins
beckoned me to come from the hungry solitude
of the room I had constructed—
"Come the Mistress of Babylon.  Drink of her wine you fornicator.
for you cannot deny you long for all her nubile gifts."

Dawn erupts in flirtatious wonder!
purples, pinks and oranges breaks through the window
with passion, exposing our flesh like cops barging into a fugitive's hovel
the motel acquiesces to the sin it hid.
And I am within it, hidden by furtive red curtains that assailed me;
pale silhouettes anointed by the dim streetlights peering in
as if to illuminate the sins I so skilfully crafted.
The carpet, red, tortured with cigarette burns—
reveals crimes long forgotten.
Black holes, a thousand eyes witnessed my profane desires
materialising as skin rustles against skin
one last time before fleeing the shadows.

4.
Then the white sheets unfurled revealing
quivering thighs, limbs, a shoulder
smooth as alabaster glistening like a departed star.
this culpable bed— these guilty furnitures
sprawled like perverts in the dark.
My senses altered to the unknown gods
whose summons we answered,
who slept here once to edify their desires.

Fallen or saved their sweat and tears remained.
The odour of the aged blankets
That once masked the dignity of infidelity
Now speaks in prophetic tongues
of the sweat they bore from perspiring limbs,
torsos, hot, colliding like planets at the formation of the universe—
perfect angles, motion rhythmic and with purpose,

directed by a hidden voyeur.
Groins groan one last time in rapturous wonder of knowing sins
now discarded within its fibres of the sheets
the immutable confessions of pimps and hookers.

"Out damn spot! If it be done, let it be done quickly!
Be like the flower, but be the serpent under it."
The particles of lovers' skins, rubbed off,
Evoke salubrious patterns in the sheets, broke the bed
in fifty different places—
-- and I tossed upon the frame.
In this unfathomable ocean of primal screams of passion
so forbidden by the prophets, yet are sweeter
sweeter than honey or even money.

And so our bodies lie limp about the aftermath, deliberate
In their ways and curves… drunken thighs
shoulders pressed into the cream walls—

All these dawn bodies worshipped together,
Incinerating entire cosmos in their hunger and fervour...

And when it was over
each ghost lingered like the strewed remains
of discarded clothes thrown away like paper, to sip more rum
add more moans to the air.

## The Whydah

*A London slave vessel that was overthrown by its captives*

Sam Bellamy was at her prow.
He'd sailed her through
many a rough seas before.
Pirate of dead men's bones
who climbed the trunk of the giant waves.
He stole the Whydah from the British Navy
stuffed his cannons with the skulls of crew:
"we'll rob even the sea of bounty,
before we're through!".

140 sea-dogs strong, ran in all directions
made ready for the brewing storm.
Below deck a young pirate eased himself out
of a deep black well, before he curses
the dance that Bacchus stomped inside
his head as sweat dripped off his
blonde wrinkled forehead.
"Never knew a negress was so silky
and nice before tonight," he admitted
to other accomplices.
burrowed his tongue into her
eyes and sought ale above deck,
up passed where the mast and sail
were frolicking under a clear moonlit night.

With the crack of whip
the Tempest's wings bellowed in the night
like horns and trumpets marching down to earth.
A thousand voices descending,
a thousand marble stairs.
The startled haulers screamed
like banshees rising from the sea
and the sails came crashing down.
"Shiver mi timbers!"
The first banner broke free
and was rend asunder
by the keen striking beam.

The Whydah, bearer of gold and silver,
180 bags in toll "more
worthy than the crew:"
Bellamy toasted and the sea-dogs
hoisted their ales
way above their drunken heads
in salute of their fiendish ways.

Unwilling passengers
black bodies snaked
in the depths of sorrow
against the dark cider of the hull,
their blood marked the terrible horror
a blood red passage they sailed
on the turbulent Atlantic.

Then drunken Captain Bellamy
read the clouds' in panic.
They gathered all around
and lightening oiled the air
and smart the wings of albatrosses
who often guided near.

Below the deck in the vast darkness,
undulating moans and groans
like the restless sea the Africans cried
as if the storm they themselves had summoned.
The unexpected cavalry laid siege
in symphony with their pleas—
they pulled and yanked their chains
calling on Shango's name.

Bellamy stomped his heels
like the crashing wine barrels upon the deck.
The slippery slope of the royal vessel,
wood and timber bend in compliance
at the behest of the sea, under bright Orion's belt.

"Calm the brutes below,
put sword to crown or throats,
for their wailing seem a-tuned
to every wicked wave

Page 62

that slams in to the Whydah's frame.
Quick men do the deed
or lose ye mangy souls to Davy Jones."

"You heard him men,
mark the Captain's will and do the deed,"
the First Mate screamed
and with ropes bound himself
to a crucial staff pole,
but with alarm he screamed and fell
the great mast came
crashing down upon his head.

And the waves congregated
in dire purpose.
No farther could they sail
though Boston's harbour was on the way
from the port bow,
not many leagues away.

The port was shrouded in the rain
and the wind rebuked with a thunderous cry
as it howled and sang the riddles
that altered the pirates' destiny
sending them down the path to hell.

No sails remained upon the vessel.
Torn and tossed asunder
her rhythm became alien to the plunderers.
"Abandon ship ye scurvy dogs!
Hark, the sea turns upon us
we are as batter for her cake.
Fetch the gold and shimmering silver.
Labour ye now, faster, faster
or taste mi iron!"

How many remained alive
or moved controlled upon the desolated deck,
Bellamy could not fathom—
but loud his baritone resounded,
like death knell's booming thunder.
One thousand slaves

shackled from their necks
to bloody ankles sore and raw—
willing accomplices of the storm.
The salt buried them under—
insolent salt would fill their lungs
to soggy death.

"Where's the gold ye women's rags?
Make ye haste and fetch what's true—
or I swear I'll run y'all through
before I'm done.
The Whydah knows I'll make ye pay!"

"Nay Cap'n, the hull is split in two!"
said a young member of the crew.
The sea has taken gold and slaves
to rest in a watery grave.
I tell ye nay, O' Bellamy,
we canna' rescue slave, gold or crew."

The pause was brief,
Bellamy made his limber way
to find the gold.
The sea regrouped for its final attack
both wave and storm inhaled
and hovered at the threshold of time
as if to remark upon the scene.

The last act of the play
where tragedy strikes its immutable blow.
And the sea in concert with the wind,
flipped the ship
and pulled it under fast and stealthily,
it took it all under,
captain and crew silenced,
removed and hidden like stolen goods
sucked to the bottom of the sea
where the wandering souls
of the captives roamed.

*Refugees*

Beneath sleepless stars, in restless nights' embrace,
When wine offers no solace, no comforting grace,
Inventions, crude or otherwise, spell men's demise,
Like an albatross leading them where death lies.

Dear readers, come with me to a realm of muses deaf,
Where Shango is blind, and Yemoja's spirit bereft,
Above well-preserved mansions, colonial relics remain,
Their zinc roofs weighed down by forgotten disdain.

Roosters crowed thrice, hens clucked in unison's plea,
Scratching at banana tree roots, oblivious and free,
Unfazed by events unfolding, unperturbed they roam,
As I set the stage for the tale of Grand-Anse, Haiti's home.

A village steeped in history, where Toussaint Louverture's might,
Once called upon heroes to stand against France's fight,
An old cannon, rusted and shrouded, lies hidden and still,
Neglected by tillers, by river gods' demanding will.

This dawn, rising from foamy depths, amidst coconut's sway,
Marks the beginning of an Odyssey, a path to convey,
Conspirators emerge from morning prayers, hearts aligned,
Honouring Yemoja and Shango, their destinies enshrined.

Esu's candles flicker, illuminating the way,
To a new world, a future where dreams hold sway,
Saint Marie, adorned with hibiscus, vibrant and fair,
Her delicate plastic skin kissed by morning's gentle air.

Now, our gaze turns inward, beyond pristine sands' gleam,
To a pomp without mirth, where morning's light may beam,
Yet souls, veiled in white, find no solace or merriment,
As white dresses twirl, heels encrusted, in psalmist lament.

Tambourines echo, slapped against hips and wrists,
As the procession meanders, through the village it persists,
Other rhythms flutter, flirtation fills the air,
Skirts dance with the breeze, folding and swirling with care.

Drawn by dreams of Haiti, I arrived, an observer's eye,
Witnessing the miraculous tale, heroes setting sail, oh my,
Forty souls in a boat, sails adorned with fins so fine,
Oars carved from oak, touched by the ocean's brine.

Ah, these men, sea-knowledge etched in their gaze,
Eyes weathered by waves, their crustacean-like haze,
Summoned by vigilant mother's thighs and fleshy arms,
Nurtured till they could venture away from her charms.

As some board the sturdy skiff, others wail and mourn,
Dancing, their spirits soar, as if wings are newly born,
The wind whispers, restless sands join the mighty dance,
White garments settle upon the lubricated expanse.

"Almighty, gaze upon the sea's vast domain,
For if your glance falters, countless lives shall wane,
Set sail swiftly upon these brine-filled waters," they plead,
Prayers bubble forth, consumed by gulls with speed.

Their pleas perfume the sea, a fragrant devotion,
Sister Andre, her head wrapped in night-like blue emotion,
Ribbons of black and white adorn her waist with grace,
Leading the village, as fish retreat, a solemn chase.

Forty heroes embarking on the unknown's embrace,
Forming a reverse ripple, defying time and space,
Their spirits united in a single black bird's flight,
Cawing from a cider perch, invaded by salt's might.

Their spirits, encapsulated within a solitary black bird's call,
Perched upon cider wood, invaded by salt's tendrils,
Unwanted remnants, a scent carried by the sea,
Goosebumps erupt, mother-woman's arms decree.

A descent of the Holy Ghost, flickering ancestral halls,
She gestures to the village, tears glistening as prayers befall,
Youth's biceps gleam, polished in the sun's hallowed hall,
Commandeering this vessel, each inch embraced before the fall.

It is a cynical journey, survival not guaranteed,

The skiff, sturdy like alpine and redwood, indeed,
Pushed by the North wind's gallant cheeks, a slow advance,
At stern and aft, port bow and hull, the mass's graceful dance.

Forty souls, men and women, dip upon this vessel's sway,
One eighth of the village, embarking on this fateful day.

O wine-dark sea, let their appeasement find its place,
Ahab and Hook, your displeasure they seek to embrace,
The plastic Sainte Marie, a buttress for their keep,
Until they reach the promised land, where speeches and wonders seep.

Hailing like circling angels, a celestial band,
They prepare for a welcome to the unpacked land,
From the ark, they alight into the arms of AUTHORITY's might,
Then to interment camps in Miami, barbed wires in sight.

They wonder at a White City, birthed from Manifest's decree,
Rome's grandchild, parapets, columns, monuments that decree,
The earth ransacked in progress's name, a plundering quest,
Marble stairs ascending, mighty lions at rest.

Paved roads, sewage systems, underground domains,
Gardens blooming with nature's reserves, a diversity of strains,
Trades bartered amidst cheating merchants' game,
Palaces ascending, confidence climbing, reaching for fame.

Channels for voice and body, wagons without steeds,
Mannequins in latest trends, their allure catching eyes like beads.

And if our Odyssey were to cease within this glass menagerie,
Quartered sidewalks, metallic din of a final gathering's spree,

What then of our journey, of this moon's revolution around the Earth?
Shall we find solace in the midst of this tumultuous mirth?

*For my dear wife Part i*

Words I send you
on the wings of Love itself—
brace yourself to receive them
tune your ears
tune your hips and toes—

Words of soothing oil
balms of spring sun shine
melodious songs of birds
I send you, O Queen of my soul—

Open up your doors
bring new linen to the table
wash your utensils
and brandish wine glasses—

Through the solitude of interstices
I come on the back of Love
from so far I've come
from such great distances—

I crossed a desert for you Darling
underneath my toes
the Nile did seem small from such heights
O sweet Nut, mother mild—

Behold a son born to woman scorned
have risen from the spoils of oppression
to love, to love and to love again
even as my enemies' faces look calculatingly—

I ride on the wings of Love
so eloquently I ride
so sweet and beguiling am I
when I steady my hips

tighten my grip
lift my face up to Heaven
and straighten my back

onward, not sideward or backward—

I skipping stone on oceans' floor
come to the door of my lover
on the wings of Love
and find her waiting with cherries at her feet.

so I bent down from Love's shoulders
and ate the cherries whole
took out my ancient papyri scroll
and wrote

a lyrical reggae song
in my native Jamaican tongue
calling upon the Rasta god
in front of my Lover—

and she understood the audible sounds
my remorseless echos
never to faded on her ears.

## Black Madonna

*of a convent with baroque altars, beamed ceilings, and a room where the nuns scourged themselves at the feet of a black Christ before the horrifying relic of a bishop's tongue, preserved in alcohol in memory of his eloquence. -Alejo Carpentier*

Behold the infinite mother tending her swarm,
Once revered, her creed a sacred form,
Yet the father and son now amiss, unseen,
Only the queen remains, the ruling sovereign.

Serenaded by infants in a tender reprieve,
Her cherubs cradle beneath, her solace they receive,
Black breasts haloed, imprisoned tears aglow,
Her sagacious virgin head, at the crucifixion's woe

A lily tongue perfumes the night's embrace,
Buoyed high, where only the sun finds its place.

Far from ancient Kush, Black Isis searches in vain,
Her betrothed wed to Serapis, the poly-god's chain,
Upon her throne, the black Madonna serene,
In Rome's Pope's presence, miracles intervene.

Yet her virginity shrouded in vile rhapsody,
Infamous nuns, pale-faced and jealous, seek to deceive,
Beckoning wolves within the flock they tend,
Lies spun for miracles before her, they pretend.

Celibacy's vows rarely spoken, children's bones broken,
Buried beneath cold stones in the nunnery's coven,
Corruption flourishes, unimaginable to behold,
Like Hypatia's murder by Cyril, in tales untold.

Her transfiguration's veil soiled, lies distort her cries,
As she nurses the demigod child, she must comport,
Peacefully sojourning in the captor's embrace,
To prepare him to avenge, falsehood's bittersweet grace.

*For my wife, Part ii*

Oh so poised at this dark window, living wife,
look on through the curtain of leaves
there I stand, a shade in your dreams—
ah! that you still wait for me to come home
from the sea with my catch on my shoulders—

thunder breaks open the mind, lightening slams
down like a judge's hammer bidding order come
and check the waves that seek to come ashore.
I toil there still, wife, though the waves alone come at my call—

I hope you do not grieve for too long
take Henry or Thomas for your husband
these men I judge still own their hearts to the tempest
and will love you and our children in earnest till we meet.

I look on through the curtains of leaves before our window
you are bound by grief in bed, it mocks your faint heart constantly.

## Child labour, the Ghetto

This scene, not meant for those of feeble heart,
Come, witness mongrels snatching babes' bone prize,
The gate to destitution lies ajar,
Plague runs amok, smoke rising to the skies.
Have youth e'er looked so defiled and forlorn?
The sight of roses bitter than the thorn.
Children in bondage to the looms they weave,
Under the watchful eyes of vile traffickers,
Their insidious lust, their victims bereave,
For defenceless souls, they're just scavengers.
Hollow men, puffed with greed, march on unmade streets,
Gathering pitiful broods ere dawn breaks bright,
Like harvesters collecting fallen seeds,
From decayed family trees, fruits of blight.
Before their tongues form speech, their hovels stand,
Locked cages, chained pegs, their world so grand.

There, she sits by a pile of syringes,
Separating nozzles from needles worn,
Washed in innocence, a cruel art lingers,
O pilot, flee this scene, this vilest scorn.
Detach yourself from this ignoble plight,
Let not this crime banish you from Life's Book,
Sleep, O sleep, till dawn's fresh light alight,
Through windows, church bells ring, halos forsaken.
Be still, the door ajar, an open gate,
The needle washer raises a hand so meek,
Unaware that your gaze did contemplate,
Her solemn labor, innocence too bleak.
Yet, in your slumber, seek a world anew,
Where needles rest, and dreams may yet come true.

## Ode to my roots

Oh, to be a tree, near a tranquil pool,
Standing tall and vibrant, keen and bright.
Beside that still, dark water I shall stay,
Upright and unwavering like a yogi in prayer,
Seeking souls to find solace beneath my branches,
Sheltering them from the relentless toil of day,
Beneath a sky woven with unspoken tales,
By the infinite pool of my solitude.

Heroes shall seek respite within my shade,
Wounded, defeated by their own battles,
Their sobs rustling through my leaves,
They do not dwell on the past,
Nor peer into the future's haze,
But remain anchored in the present,
Just standing in their place,
Between Heaven's heights and Hell's depths,
Between sleep's embrace and wakefulness,
Basking under the sun's warm glow,
Finding solace in the fragrance of my blossoms.

Silent observer, with a power both sure and enchanting,
Content in stillness, a witness to pilgrims' journeys,
Ascending and descending like angelic beings,
Upon Jacob's ladder, they find respite and repose,
At my cool black pool, where truths are baptized,
Shared in a communion of common understanding.

*Double consciousness*
*(or skin lightening cream)*


To the most evangelical,
whitening is a way of life
dancing with mercury
under a pale moonlit night.
Its quick-silver tongue gives
a brief taste of the illusion
of white purity—

Whiteness comes with a price.
To the god Hydroquinone, a sacrifice
for a fleeting reward – for many
lightening is worth the risk of cancer
having no defence against the UV rays
produced by the Heavenly eye above.

They wage a silent war
against the diabolical skin, liver and kidney
strips of darkness folds like plastic
and peeled from their arms, torsos and legs
like Christmas presents unwrapped
with childish wonder— a pale yellow layer
of membrane gleams in the darkness
with chills of satisfaction.
Alas the ugliness is chiseled away.
A new marble sculpture is displayed
like Michael Angelo's David,
confident with grace.

They are taught to be ashamed
of the melanin they are born with
the melanin embroidered in their skin—
ceremoniously they kill the Melanin God within
scrubbing off the primordial slug
to find acceptance, success!
In the image of their former masters,
remade—a white alabaster Venus De Milo
with a moonlike complexion.

Light skin is the mark of privilege
power and contentment.
When you're "fair and lovely"
all doors are open.
Brighter, smarter more honest,
are qualities the dark skinned one's
cannot aspire— they bay with wolfish envy,
with sly sidelong glances
and ridicule rolls off their tongues
as pure white bliss escapes them.
They cover their faces with ashes
because to them you have conquered—
rose from the pit of darkness and despair
bright and pure like snow.

Forced albinism, hidden in shade—
dark mahogany idols hacked to pieces
from colonised thoroughbred stallions,
persecuting black Diablo, the accursed.

The fair skinned ones are the lighthouses
in poor Cape Town, Kingston, Jamaica—
where the offsprings
of "Ham" are afflicted and assailed
by the curses of Melanin?

## Rebirth of a Nation

In the blazing sun, our bodies ache and burn,
Faces branded, scars that never seem to turn.
Torn from our mothers' arms, lost and roaming,
Seeking a home, in this world we keep on owning.
Are we fading away, caught in this cruel game?
We rise above the pain, gotta find our own fame.

(Chorus)
From the ashes we'll rise, no compromise,
Through struggle and strife, we claim our own lives.
In this unjust world, we'll fight and we'll strive,
Unbreakable spirits, we won't be denied.

Lashes slice our backs, the pain never ends,
But we won't let it break us, we'll make amends.
Unrequited prisoners, oppressed and confined,
But our voices will be heard, no longer confined.
Turbulent waves crashing, like serpents at our feet,
But we rise above, won't accept defeat.
No curse can hold us down, we're breaking free,
In our hearts and minds, we'll rewrite history.

(Chorus)
From the ashes we'll rise, no compromise,
Through struggle and strife, we claim our own lives.
In this unjust world, we'll fight and we'll strive,
Unbreakable spirits, we won't be denied.

Snowflakes fall, a cold and icy embrace,
But we're not frozen, we'll win this race.
Our minds are sharp, our resilience strong,
We'll prove them wrong, keep pushing along.
Cotton fields surround us, where we once toiled,
But we'll rise above, our dreams won't be spoiled.
We're more than commodities, we're kings and queens,
In this democratic hell, we'll shatter the scenes.

(Chorus)
From the ashes we'll rise, no compromise,
Through struggle and strife, we claim our own lives.

Page 77

In this unjust world, we'll fight and we'll strive,
Unbreakable spirits, we won't be denied.

(Bridge)
This is our anthem, our battle cry,
We won't be silenced, we'll touch the sky.
We stand united, strong and bold,
Breaking barriers, stories yet untold.

(Chorus)
From the ashes we'll rise, no compromise,
Through struggle and strife, we claim our own lives.
In this unjust world, we'll fight and we'll strive,
Unbreakable spirits, we won't be denied.

(Outro)
We're writing our story, rewriting the game,
No more shackles, we'll never be the same.
In the face of adversity, we'll always stand tall,
Unleashing our power, breaking down every wall.

Page 79

## Oil 2001, Nigeria

*For Ken Saro Wiwa hanged in 1995 by the military dictatorship of General Sani
Abacha for protesting Shell's exploitation of the Niger Delta region.*

(Spoken Word Performance)

A poet is dead!
A rusty black god took his final breath at 9am,
And our mourning faces tell the tale.
Wildflowers frown, their heads bent low,
Their stems soaked in the stench of oil.
Oh Anansi, black spider,
Messenger and storyteller in the 8th Sphere,
Behold the devastation!
Our poet is dead?

Yes, O Lord, his blood spills,
Mixing with the black gold of this land.
White ghosts hide behind Yoruba, Ebo, and Hausa masks,
While our black kings parade from parliament,
Like jesters on gentrified horses.

The ground quakes with our pain,
Rattling as we unleash our wails.
Where are the bones of the oil warriors?
Those slain by Chevron's AK-47s,
Their lives traded for monetary gains,
Their corpses filling barrels,
Carried away by tankers to American soil.

Witness the carnage.
See where yams made their final stand.
See the imprisoned souls of poverty.

The business of blood
Displays the oil king's face,
Upon the round table of despair.

But the poet's blood is with us!
It fuels us, like a fiery force.
The poet's blood will propel us!

Burn it in the lamps on writing desks.
Ignite the tiresome city
With the power of his oily flesh!

Today is a day of tears and suffering,
So let the poet's blood ignite your gatherings!
Create bonfires with that martyred blood!
Let the sonorous drums resound!

And let a trail, as long as the Nile,
Be marked with the oil that stole countless lives.
Use your matches and your guns,
Resurrect flames in the poet's blood...

## Song for my African son

Welcome back home, my son, it's been too long,
Rest your head upon my knee, where you belong.
You were wild, flippant, arrogant and free,
Now let me trace the scars of hate that I see.
Your face hardened by the ravages of time,
Torn by white fragility, it's a painful climb.
But I'm here to nurse the wounds, ease your pain,
Take off the burden of police brutality's strain.

Tell me 'bout your journeys through racism's minefields,
How did you survive, with the weight that it yields?
The school to prison pipeline, what did it take,
To escape the hate, the walls that they make?
In what jail did you pray, longing for release,
Haunted by the sirens of indelible white lies?
Your history rewritten, your genocide televised,
To unsympathetic eyes, the world just turns a blind eye.

(Chorus)
And who revived you, my black child, my ebon' son?
Was it the stoic gun's loaded stare or silence on the run?
Your bed's unchanged, Kaffir boy, washed in the River Jordan,
Outside your window, grass still green, hope's horizon.
Come and sit with me, wanderer of killing fields,
Western imperialist dreams, fantasies that won't yield.
Spread your arms out for landing, your journey's done,
Welcome back, embraced by African brothers, my son.

In the arms of your betrayers, find solace and strength,
Among your sleeping African kin, your heritage's length.
It's a complex reunion, history's deep divide,
But we stand united, together side by side.
Embrace the revolution, let the ghetto fade away,
Your homecoming's a symbol, a brighter, better day.

(Outro)
Welcome back, my son, you've endured so much strife,
But through it all, you've found the power to thrive.
The hip hop beats, they echo your voice,
A testament to resilience, a triumph, a choice.

Embrace your roots, your strength, your African pride,
For you are home now, where love will reside.

## The Buccra[2]

Mawoba embraced his steed's weary head,
Close to his heart, in sorrow it bled.
On the plains, silent and low,
He mourned the loss, his tears did flow.

Confused and aware, he faced the truth,
His faithful companion, a life now uncouth.
No time to dig a hole in the ground,
He hid the steed, his loyal hound.

Arrows scabbarded on his shoulder's right,
Mawoba ventured into the forest's night.
Rain interrupted his anguished cries,
But he pressed on, determination in his eyes.

He dragged the steed to a hidden grove,
Concealing it from the beats that rove.
With vines and sticks, he marked the way,
To navigate the forest, where darkness lay.

Into the depths, Mawoba tread,
To slay the beast, Buccra, born of dread.
Spawned from Albion, a creature of Hell,
A tale of vengeance, he sought to tell.

With puffs of breath, his chant began,
A warrior's song, a Ntambo clan.
It resonated through the rain-filled trees,
Calling forth strength, dispelling unease.

"Blue tablecloth of Juluba,
Protect my eyes, tempered fire,
In blade clashes, I shall see,
Buccra's paw, his armour dire.
Arrows sharp, I'll cut him down,
With Juluba's cloth, I'll wear victory's crown."

---

[2] *Jamaican Patois for slave master.*

The forest surrounded, a daunting sight,
Mahoganies watched, tall and tight.
Mawoba, guided by Juluba's cloth,
Rain-soaked and barefoot, he ventured forth.

Buccra's lair, adorned with death's embrace,
Skulls and entrails, a haunting place.
A pile of bodies, limbs and gore,
Ntambo babies torn, their lives no more.
Mawoba's tears flowed at the sight,
His toes crumpled, weighed down by the fight.

Wounded and sly, Buccra lay,
A trail of blood marking his way.
Mawoba armed his arrows true,
Ready to confront the beast he knew.

In Buccra's lair, amidst the fog,
Mawoba charged, a heroic slog.
His bow tightened, arrows in flight,
A warrior's fury, his final fight.

Buccra, startled, turned to see,
The gallant warrior, fierce and free.
Arrows flew, in perfect sync,
Impaling the beast, a deadly link.

Buccra, in pain, rose on hind legs,
Attempting escape, his body begs.
But missteps and rain hinder his stride,
As arrows pierce him, death defied.

With a final howl, Buccra fell,
The layer shook, a mournful knell.
Mawoba wasted no time in delay,
Upon the fallen beast, he made his way.

With one last arrow, he took aim,
Raindrops fell, his heart aflame.
Four hundred years of terror in mind,
He plunged the arrow, fate unkind.

Into Buccra's eyes, the arrow sank,
The epic battle, Mawoba's victory to thank.
The putrid lair rattled, filled with woe,
As Mawoba avenged, dealt the final blow.

*Forty days and forty nights*

**Written in Lagos, Nigeria, Saturday October 13, 2001**

Alone— you must drink loneliness
loneliness thirst for what you carry—
alone— you must go alone
loneliness will go with you
until the sorrowful crows
bewitch you with their eyes
and you must eat the snails you find
raw… raw is your throat
on that day the journey undertakes you
and takes you alone
borne on the gentle wings of silence
to the lair of loneliness

Pack nothing—
hear the avid verses of lost poets
there upon the winds?
They utter Loneliness' motto and creed—
take no belongings
one pair of sandals should be enough
one robe of simple threads
there to greet Loneliness in his abode
to eat his flames and live
"Why have you come?" he will inquire slow
and unscathed,
your eyes the candles of the lost
will utter your design
and even Loneliness will leave you standing on a precipice
    lamenting like an unhappy bride
    as temptation attends you
    and inflicts your flesh with boils
    that desert trees are accustomed ~

But loneliness carries love as ancient as the royal sky
that drinks in remembrance of you—
so please you have come to test the might of solitude.

Forty days and forty nights
without a mortal fire

in the company of rocks and stones
in the palm of knowledge, a wasteland
with petulant shrubs,
which eyes you and bites you
the first chance they get ~

Soon hours have fallen victim to your game,
minutes fly and seconds leap like embers
from the surface of your bones and face—
Teasing desert, curious breezes adorn your feet with pity ~
Hours where have you gone?
Hours when will you return?

What day is this?
A coiled snake of lock hangs upon a wild brow
hunger says its own name
and ran-sacked the belly
the morning sky dances like a belly dancer in an opium den,
morose ears expel the wicked laughter of scorpions
that pleads with you to stroke them in your palms ~

Silence becomes echo, echo wars with silence
and days become infinite like the snake
that bid, "kill and eat.
I am yours,
kill and eat."

In the blossoming night the hours return.
Twilight wants blood.
The hours return
and temptation is upon the winged lion
coming out of the belly of the sky with permission
        to kill.

What day is this?
What hour glares from heaven?

--recoiling body stretched out upon the sand
as waves of heat marauds the land.
Out of the cave of darkness,
night steps forth into flesh, stands by the mouth of the cave
like a widow—waiting for her turn to swallow

your remaining hours, days,
the seconds leaped from your brows
as trickling sweat rolling into your eyes
down your cheeks like petrified rabbits.

II      **Water in the cave**

The dark indomitable pool spake unto you
as you meditated into nothingness
touching the coat-tail of infinity
engulfed by eternal peace and a bliss
you never knew existed before summoned
you into the depths where only spirits
may sojourn, to be lost forever

Somehow one day, a thousand
billion hours ago it divided into two—
that pool, in the furthest reaches of your mind
and now it has no memory of you
soon you will have no memory of its existence
in the shape of a homo sapient.

Prayers lubricate your dry sandy lips,
new lovers emerged from the pit
savouring each kiss for hours
salvation flows down her arch back
salvation cries out in birth pains
salvation is the hunger in your belly
the demon you wrestled with
that hid its name on your tongue
salvation comes when she adorned your locks
salvation is the still hunger on the Sabbath.

The cave hears the echos of the Messiah
coming to greet the transfigured body it housed
so secretly like single minded bird
folded over its shivering young
so it opens its shadowy places
the cave spoke in many tongues
the cave burns with the footprints of the Christ
carved into its smooth cool stone body
it kicks out and screams out

a priestess sees through smoke and bones.

and silence comforts you
silence calls out to loneliness
and loneliness melts your heart with kisses
soft and enigmatic
it admits it never meant   to tease you
tempt you to fear the      god within
to abandon your        totems—
madness retreats,          death's coin upon its
tongue.
The hour removed its      veil and revealed
cyclical time sitting in     judgement..

Your feet of burnished      bronze
meandered to the sea
wooly hair ablaze, a               black
burnished afro
the hair coils             upon itself as time
reciting its        wicked rhymes to a child
fingers         joined each other on the back of
your bony         hands,
veins cry for       mercy, the
neck a stiff       post
thankfully       starving
and smiling
gently         into the face
of God.

**III The first step**           **upon the**
**wave**

   The         back is           an open
field
brown                     barren
land of flesh
  the spine glories           in the light
  of the word           embracing flesh
              (and Jehovah walks in)
         the backs of both heels split into
        three places
        heels, cracked old walls

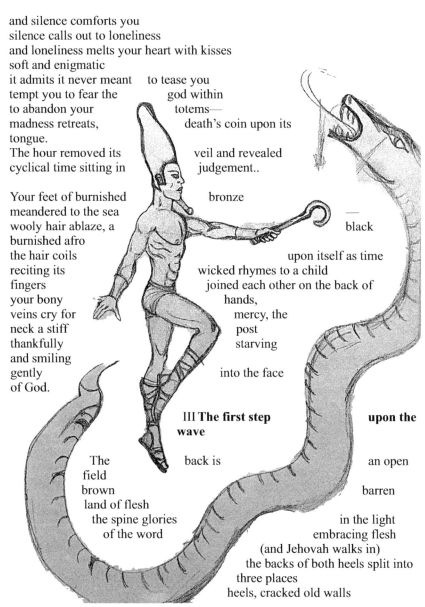

legs of burning pillars from antiquity
pyramids sprout from your collar bones
as your prayers are dispersed into molecules
and atoms and electrons and protons and neutrons
                              (and Jehovah walks in)
prayers jumped from your lips
became smoke and sweet odours of incense offering
sweat beads up and roll down your sloped iron cheeks

                              (and Jehovah walks in)
cherubim dream of elevating the humming flow.

They spiral downward with pleasant tidings
they come to your call
the whole cave becomes chiming leaves awoken by a virgin gust.
He calls out your ren[3]
and you blossomed in many places.
Sweat falls to the ceiling.
"He speaks in the tongues of the Holy Spirit?"
Does he make himself before us with mere words?
He calls flesh and bones and sinews from the void
"Let light become." Building each bone out of air.

The sea turns its pages like a fortune teller
spreading her deck of cards before the querent
the sand mutely warns
the current of the ocean carries
a breath of fresh air soft as silence
your toes take root in the sands of hours
morning long eclipsed by inquisitive stars
magnets pole their position in your begotten blood.

Your name is in all things—
you are the wings of the falcon
soaring above the heaving tumultuous sea
you are the dragon of creation
Leviathan humbles before your spear and thrust
remaking yourself in yourself
you are your own mirror of delight.

Everywhere your name resounds like an echo
a physical name, a purposeful being
not stranded by time, you inflicted tongues upon the breeze,
sea and sand—

"Be still— I made you
do not elapse, do not weaver,
suspend your motion
I know your nature
The coils in your springs
I beseech you with my utterances."

---

[3] *The word for name in Ancient Egypt.*

Sand slid into the waves
your hems folded, wet, upon your thin calves
and buoyancy is achieved—
the abysmal water has become solid under your feet
the apex of the waves were like small mounds under your toes
the hammering from below had ceased
like when a storm has abated suddenly.
You marvelled in death
rejected the calculations of life
and walked as a mastodon upon the waves.


## IV *Casting out demons*

*And when he was come to the other side into the country of the Gergesenes,*
*there met him two possessed with devils, coming out of the tombs, exceeding*
*fierce, so that no man might pass by that way. —Matthew 8:28-34*

arguments erupted upon the sands—
rocks with murderous teeth—
wet appetites,
the joyful heart of the surfs
is elated and content

the quarrelsome sea-wind
hustled up the bank
like a Roman chariot
a blazing shield of unforgiving memories
was the sun

a prophetic hour had come
he was expecting a sunny day
the sky vertigoes in the expanse over the sea
in blushing haze of oranges and light yellows

flowing white linen of Heaven
clouds with palms like wailing virgins
still, silent, soundless as a Roman chariot
shoots out like an arrow
as it passes a petrified cave

he was expecting rest
and visitations
he had to eat before the voyage
the sea ogled at the Messiah and recoiled,
a faithful pet watching its master
who's on the verge of divinity

he wanted unleavened bread before the voyage..
the sea ogled him and bowed
like a sycophant at court
clouds like palmed virgins gracefully dispersed
as the bridegroom approached—

as the cave shifts perspective
            a shadow erupted to confront the word
That had become flesh

the cave dweller was startled by his footsteps
like a hyena transfixed by a lion
it pleaded with the hills
"Hide me, I beg you.." the hill responded,
"Truth is persistence when all is lost
nothing is hidden from him."

The host wailed and thrashed upon the ground
and beat its chest in defiance
"Why have you come forth from the desert
with speeches
to turn stone into bread?!"

the visitor motioned into the air to the swinish form
that was not itself
blind, contorted facial expressions
knuckles of blood dragged along the gravelled path
lips bruised with stones
eyes like cracked mirrors
reflects unnatural habitations within..

a winnowing howl burst forth
from the harsh throat of the cave dweller
as if to confess forgotten lies
satanic verses babbled off his tongue

saliva darted like venom
and his countenance was wild and beastly
he was a wild dance of errors
moving gingerly on his filthy toes

is this how demons tread in men's bodies?
a dark ministry presides within
a choir of defiance conducted
by the great serpent god
who dared to steal the light
a motherless hunger consumes
an agent of famine moons
who rides upon the backs of locusts
the empty sack of the reaper
discarded on the rocky road
his corpse ten feet hence
the outcast's immortal rage,
festering from the dawn of time
suns flung in righteous anger
across the emptiness of between galaxies
in rebellion— with hubris —
the bitterness of the fallen has met its equal
that inhabits this body—

"Hail Satan, bringer of sorrow
you will never find peace in the bushes
or in the brothels, or in this cave
nor in Lebanon's olive groves"—
The messiah spoke with the tongue
of the hushed sea beneath him

"suffer us to inhabit the swines"
the twisted jaws pleaded—
The Christ, burnish black
with feet of bronze
eyes like smouldering embers
commanded the fallen go

a multitude of voices hushed out into the air,
like a cyclone devouring
the innocence of the suffering land
vying for supremacy in the morning star

Page 95

their formless bodies a plummeting sacrifice
and no one saw but the little swineherd
his squealing pigs fled from him
headed towards the hungry cliffs
and tumbling like boulders
crashing into the hunger sea

the redeemed cave dweller
rose from the gravelled path
and meandered silently
into the ebony arms of the Messiah
and he was hugged like a new born child
his pale body inhaled sharply
as his divine nature long forgotten
came flooding back into the hollow corpse
it once discarded.

*Sermon on a minibus to Lagos*

Prayers, a descending escalator of water
rushing over the tongue of our man,
who knows how to take us
in the company of his words—
a railing horse that throws and gallops
into a Moorish sunset.

He makes us docile little lilies
in an old garden box.
The horse's eyes move frantically at prayer
we fold ourselves in recognition
of the imminent cherubim.

Chorus: "Ahmi—ahmi
our flesh is substantiated by god
we do not corrode like untended iron in rain."

He oils each of us with prayers.
We flex our joints in recognition.
Our heads, like the egress crane's
the erudite bird of Egypt
and in the soup thick silence
for just one moment,
a woman's cracked dirt caked fingers
alighted onto her left collar bone
with the remembrance of contracted wings.

Chorus: "Ahmi—ahmi!"

## In Africa nature takes

Gather her gifts from shattered halls,
Tattered pages and worn-out walls.
Cracked clay and bullet-marked decay,
Whispered tales of yesterday.

She plays no favorites, this relentless force,
Demanding sacrifice from every source.
She claims her rights, all things in her domain,
From every fragment, she reclaims.

Her army of ants and termites, they march,
As soil and vines entwine, they embark.
With tendrils around your throat, they squeeze,
Challenging your ego, bringing you to your knees.

Schools crumble with a single touch,
White walls, stale and dry, not much.
She counts her students, slouching graves,
A confrontation, her message engraves:
"I am your greatest challenge, you see,
To live, you must tame and circumvent me.
These American books, a foreign breed,
They belong elsewhere, another need."

The terrain is her element, her domain,
A single limb breathing, a deep humming refrain.
She hunches like a crone, carrying you away,
Everything you see, hers to sway.
Unconcerned for the weak and frail,
She roams freely, her will prevails.

The wanderer bends to her commanding voice,
Her words aligned with destiny's choice.
Heads roll, calabashes bounce on her spine,
As she leads with stagnant water's sign.

Unmarked stones and human scents,
Reach their limit, the trail ends.
Her animals slip away, sly and keen,
Into the dense jungle, unseen.

When men approach, they disappear,
Her wisdom surpasses what modern minds revere.

So be sure to swallow the bravery you seek,
For the moving waters, mighty and meek.
The spoils of her victories left to decay,
Neglected offspring along the way.

## Mustard seed

*fBehold, I tell thee this truth:*
*Even as a grain of mustard seed,*
*If thy faith be as small as this,*
*Thou shalt command the mountain to move,*
*And it shall be moved,*
*For naught is impossible to thee.*

*In but an hour it shall not sprout,*
*Yet within minutes thou canst nurture it,*
*If thou practiceth mindfulness,*
*Like swallows in the shrubs.*
*It doth plant its roots within thy mind,*
*This parable, my friend, is a seed,*
*Sown gently by the idle breeze,*
*Its power is the key,*
*To unlock the mountains,*
*Those obstacles that render thee human,*
*At the crossroads of life.*

*Mountains shall tremble before the seed,*
*A deliberate mace of fury,*
*Plucked from the trees,*
*Heralded by bees and butterflies,*
*Over lilies and ferns,*
*Through the embracing trees.*
*A clear mission it brings,*
*For all to perceive and know.*

*This humble mustard seed,*
*If cultivated, cherished, and believed,*
*Shall cause great oceans to grieve,*
*For all to partake, like holy communion.*
*Place it upon thy tongue,*
*As a precious silk pearl.*
*Angels plant it within children,*
*And fate is powerless against it.*

*Blessed virgin of Ethiopia*

The Virgin sits with her begotten son
full of tranquility and adoration
upon her head a crown of precious stones.

Your words greeted my heart
like palm wine freshly brewed in Ife
by old women in aprons,
heads tied in damp hot weather.

Dear friend of the griot,
as my throat finds its choir again,
and nightingales perch on my windowsill
and tweet with glee for me and above my head,

near my delectable pillow made by R L,
cotton sacks, silently observing:
the Blessed Black Virgin of Ithiopia looks on,
her eyes gently stroking my face with mercy.

And then I bowed down in reverence and joy
begging to be free of ploys,
and though I judge myself harshly at times,
I pity my soul, dragged as it has been
by my ego through bars in the East Village.

Prayer takes me like the flicker of a candle
on a hair of the wind.
Reconciled and divinely challenged
I dissipated onto the floor like dust and remained still
my double consciousness expunged
as I prostrated myself before the Black Virgin.

## Lovers quarrel

Today I held her and she whispered, "It will rain."
Soft tears coagulated like dew in my embrace
almost miraculously she communicated her pain
the sorrow under her eyes spilled their remains.

"It will rain"-- and seabirds over our heads echoed
sentiments of her words far away, they took her sorrow.
A moth trapped between windowpanes of tomorrow
asked what doom does the rain intends for sparrows.

It will never know the answer.
It will only remember the heavy consistent murmur
rhythm of ice hitting the ground as we decide to surrender
our love for one another, the sky look on in wonder.

It understands lovers' quarrels are washed away in the rain
Its an unremarkable pain that is felt everyday.
We search for oneness with another like shopping for games
But soon we are left standing alone serenaded by the rain.

*Message in a bottle— Coney Island*

The content of your breath has expired—
all the sand you have swallowed
recalled the first muse at your lips
sipping what you hold within--
a child's first satin dress you stained
left entangled in a cornfield filled with rain.
—Dusty bottle gazing, the circus behind
is without pomp or life.
The cold has driven the pedestrians away—
but stand you here alone
with transparent shoulders
an iconoclast by my ankles
companion to the first shard excavated in France
as if you discovered the coast
where our sea nurses
for a lover, or a son—
the anonymous maker who held you
one fraction of a second—
sand does its best to fill you—
the Coney Island water nests within—
when we are dead you will be
our proof of advanced life on earth—
the sea hauls itself unto the sand like a seal—
all for you, container of castaway memoirs.
Pope of bottles—
I unravel you from within
I strode with you once.

## Orpheus

Divine reed within this black reclining body,
O' heart full as wine, I pour you out for the visitors
who have come to hear my intestines plucked
by fingers of the dreaded one—in dreaming darkness.

Alas my ribs removed and cast into Hephaestus's fire,
that abandoned  angel worked my body into a slender brown flute
with gold perfection, fashioned I, from the hollow stem—

Send him word, my Orpheus!
could he rescue me from the graveyard of Titans?
their machinations and cunning machines lead us like the Pied Piper
from the old neighbourhood to deep and sunless hell.

When am returned to my proper place, man and beast united
the tree within shall extend its roots out to the deep hearts core
linnets wings below the chin shall breathe fresh air into these lungs,
sweet tears for thirsty cups, I bring.

## The flute player's dead child

Often at mornings when the beds are of stones
he comes and shares the lyre's truth
reminds that song is perfect
like crisp leaves firm in spring.

A vase hums in the humid aftermath
its tongue, the flickering red curtain over a mahogany bench—
rose petals flat on their backs stared
up at the mouth that held them for only hours.
They die with soft playing

learned to sing to soothe the dead girl.
The stones will be soft linen again
when she dances with thankful teasing
knowing for her it was constructed—

for her the melody did not stray
until the stone gave way
and she            stepped
out of the songs between void.

Page 106

## Meo, Sept 96, Saarbrücken, Germany

We reaped the squashes and onions together.
I black bard from Harlem and she
an old German woman.
Eighty-seven unfathomable years,
never needing spectacles to see, never once without
the space of a garden except perhaps
during the war after Konig Ludwig II's fairy tale death.

Breathing softly with steel sheers she dragged herself
accurately among patches of reds and lime grass,
a small marijuana plant is hidden by a grandson who is married
to a cloud that is thin and rakes the ground
She cuts around the ganja plant, like a one hundred year old botanist.
Nothing is supposed to die in her garden.

Tending the garden, a dead husband's grave she has never seen,
only imagined. Clipping the dead leaves from every living plant.
meticulously breathing she bends lower till her breasts touched
her strong knees.

Showing no signs of weariness, she returned to a reclining chair
nearby-- slowly sitting-- she muttered something melodious in German
then closing her almost transparent eye lids in the dim sunlight.
When I wanted to hear war stories she gave me tea in ancient cups
without cracks, as if to say here is the history you requested young man.
Thinking of what should have been the grave of her husband.

His whole garrison was never buried. Scattered remains forgotten?
A patriot defending the Reich. No strings attached.
Fighting for Germany is costly even now. He was one of those
solders, who kindly killed the Jews.

Decades ago she lived with Jews in Temmels near the boarder
of Luxembourg. She spoke to Jews, Jews spoke to her.
She was silent knowing her husband might
not return from the cold heart of Russia.
She bought their memories when no one would, if just to cry into them.
Tea cups and saucers were all she could fit into her apron.
They tell such great stories when memories are dying.

## Gardens of Ramallah

### *for children of Palestine*

Ransacked gardens left untended
wailing stones cry freedom,
wailing silence breaks bones of children,
like twigs snapping under stomping boots—
humans combust like confetti—
the displaced bodies gathered bullets like peas,
children of war crashed like waves
against the great wall of Jerusalem.

Gardens of Ramallah watered
with the blood of children:
Sami Jazzar shot in the head
by an Israeli soldier
on the eve of his 12th birthday in Gaza;
11 year-old Khalil Mugharbi,
killed by Israeli sniper in Gaza.
"John doe" survived, shot in the testicles
by a high velocity round;
10 year-old Riham al-Ward,
killed in her Jenin schoolyard
by an Israeli tank shell:
Which child does Netanyahu love?

They fall like logged trees
in a forest tucked away from humanity
fleeing from the Zionist usurpers.
The children like boulders
firmly planted in the river of flowing blood--
the weeds of isolation gathered in gardens
as the malaise of fever grows
into weeds of vengeance and suicide bombings.
There is terror in Gethsemane
the Earth cleansed of her children
wailing mothers begged
for the lives of their children
prayers go unanswered in the endless shelling.

## Chronicle of an eye

Thirsty vulture, with yearning in its swoop,
Desperate, stalking its prey with intent.
Summoned by dark winds, it writes a strange loop,
Etching messages on faces, lines well-spent.

If we could speak the language of the breeze,
Plain it would be, from Afghanistan it came,
Witnessing a young girl's stoning, unease,
For she dared to remove her sacred veil's frame.

Or perhaps it hails from Katmandu's land,
Where hundreds left homeless by monsoon's might,
Seek refuge atop roofs, where they now stand,
Awaiting respite from nature's relentless fight.

It may have traveled to Ethiopia's realm,
Stirring up sand 'mongst starving villagers,
Reckless and out of sync, causing o'erwhelm,
Disrupting lives, like callousness of pillagers.

This busy eye, a witness to it all,
Touring the world, God's heart it observes,
Even in deepest Africa's nightfall,
It seeks and sees, as darkness it deserves.

Machetes, in tribal fray, take deep bites,
Carving wounds on black bodies in their strife,
This eye reveals, with each blustering flight,
The scenes of anguish, speaking life's harsh fife.

Whistling and howling, the eye's speech prevails,
Conveying tales in bluster, fierce and clear,
A witness to the world's relentless trails,
Its messages, for all attentive ears to hear.

*Harlem NY, a homeless winter*

Such chilling news winter brings,
A red ribbon is cut to welcome the jittery bones of cold.
Windows buckled shut for a millennia to come,
A key breaks in a lock, an elevated train slinky over our heads.
A K-9 sniffs the history of human skin.

We curled up in our soft rooms like hibernating animals,
Content in warmth and irrelevant notes,
Unaware of those who beat the snow until their fingers froze,
Friends to icicles and slippery roads.

She sleeps in a box in winter's wake,
A fool, but what if you had no cozy room?
Had to brave the crowded shelters "between sleep and wake",
Teased with the aroma of the destitute's unwashed bodies.

Spirited away in life's painful inexorable rapids,
Scarcely in the tumult of their suffering,
Gentle hands outstretched in countless rows of beds.
Where sleep and wake dance haphazardly on a fragile thread.

*Woman in 2G, Amsterdam Ave*

sings the blues to herself and
wonders about the moon's
unusual medicine.
How its grains of light
just seem to float
like humid air over the eye-
lids of generation X smoking
pot and cigarettes below her spotless sill.
It seems so solemn as it stares.
Cold, invisible smiles on to the tar;
on the gravelled roof unfurnished
with rejected bottles of Colt 45s,
tired Budweiser cans mangled
in disgust or satisfaction;
murdered Marlborough butts lay twisted
like distorted bodies extinguished
for naught but their complacency.
The voices of generation X are loud and harsh
like a garrison blocking the entrance
to the woman's red brick
apartment in Harlem.
Like idle sentinels laughing at
anyone who dared approach them--
and it is when you are approaching
that in their mocking smiles
you can see the pulsating disdain for authority
the smell of a smirking gun pointing at your head
spinning tales from the dreaded hood,
eager for a mystery the moon
refuses to disclose in Harlem.

## The Dunblane Massacre

*An elegy for the 16 innocent children and 1 teacher killed in the Dunblane Primary school massacre 1996 in Scotland*

**I**

Imagine a colourful classroom humming
hushed chatter between friends—
the rustling of pages, lined with discipline—
the smell of rubber burning to erase errors.
Imagine little hands shooting up into the air
like Icarus soaring too close to the sun
eager to please their teacher, excited hearts.
Now imagine an invasion of bullets devouring
their flesh like the Black Death.

The innocence of childhood crumpled.
A deranged assassin, a prowling wolf,
a heartless pig, snatching their souls like trophies.
They say he shouldn't own guns though he carried 4

The miraculous things white privilege can do..
boys who he photographed chest bared
frightened like puppies somewhere in the past.

Their puzzled eyes like scurrying rabbits.
My foreign eyes overflowing with anger.
Their white unblemished skin pleading to live—
the white terrorist armed to the teeth with death
baptising the innocent with hollow tip confessions.
White on white violence so cold and calculating.
The television says he was blond perfection
He was a lone gunman, no affiliation.

I walked on my soles in the valley of death.
The souls of the dying beckoned me with harrowing faces.
The angel they've learnt to scorn.
Even hate my black skin.
Hating me for screaming 'No!' on their simple graves.
God, am I loving them.
My soul screamed in agony as their tears
Lacerated my skin, lacerated the air I breathed

lacerated the throat that uttered psalms.

Their prized white hands lifeless
lifeless expressions on canvas—
white cherubs fallen from their Picasso clouds.
I am the god of broken promises, guarding them is my right.
I shed mine like feathers falling from an eagle
soaring above the chickens running for cover.
Skins are a dime a dozen ---

## II

He spoke to his guns like they were his children
armed himself with four,
walked into a primary school gym and
started shooting. 700 bullets...
firing at random killing and injuring
children—five—six— before he turned
the gun on himself. That's what the Mirror said.
That's the tale of the magic mirror
you look hard enough your true self appears
twisted, and fiendish like an imp,
a gargoyle ogling its deformed ugliness.

No one was safe from the eye of the gun
spinning as if in a dance as they fell—
her prayers turned to blood, her pleas
lost forever in the vengeance of a so called "mad man"
no not terrorist even though he planned
struck terror and fear in the hearts of 16 innocent little ones.
No not terror, for his whiteness cannot be tarnished
even though he attacked and destroyed
the sweet nectar of childhood
Scattered bees to the wind like dust.

The media ventriloquists adept with deception said:
"he was ostracised at school struggling
with accusations that he was strange and was a paedophile."
Does this mean his actions were somehow justified?

I am the foreign witness, I know your crimes
the ambassador of pain and suffering
embarrass to see me you cringed like Sméagol –

my eyes lost in a brew of tears.
I tell tales -- I steal lives
transmitted from across the Atlantic
to touch me deep with invisible inaudible comma splices.
You fabricated fake news to save the propaganda of your skin.

Forgetting the teacher who folded like a blanket
beckoning the lost souls to her arms.
She could promise nothing but prayer sentences.
Exclamations of impotence.
I watched from behind crossed fingers, timing the wrath.
Hearts opened like pomegranates,
as he terrorised the weakest among them
payment for his family's shame.

Halos shall shatter in darkness, mountains shall sink into the sea
as you protect the monsters with white skin
the Frankensteins you've created haunts your dreams
as their reality is far too real for you to keep it hidden.

Printed in Great Britain
by Amazon

c5ea45a9-2585-4b6d-908c-4610339a00d5R01